T0354509

THE STRUGGLE

THE STRUGGLE

MATEMA MAGAGANE

authorHOUSE®

AuthorHouse™
1663 Liberty Drive
Bloomington, IN 47403
www.authorhouse.com
Phone: 1-800-839-8640

© *2012 by Matema Magagane. All rights reserved.*

No part of this book may be reproduced, stored in a retrieval system, or transmitted by any means without the written permission of the author.

Published by AuthorHouse   07/10/2012

ISBN: 978-1-4670-0024-6 (sc)
ISBN: 978-1-4670-0025-3 (e)

Any people depicted in stock imagery provided by Thinkstock are models, and such images are being used for illustrative purposes only.
Certain stock imagery © Thinkstock.

This book is printed on acid-free paper.

Because of the dynamic nature of the Internet, any web addresses or links contained in this book may have changed since publication and may no longer be valid. The views expressed in this work are solely those of the author and do not necessarily reflect the views of the publisher, and the publisher hereby disclaims any responsibility for them.

CONTENTS

THIS IS A MEMOIR

While based on true events and my recollections, they may not coincide with what others depicted in the story experienced or remember.

Therefore, in consideration of that fact and in the interest of protecting privacy, all names, relationships, locations, incidental characters, and situations were changed, altered or occasionally fictionalized in order to conceal identities.

Some dramatic effect might occur to better illustrate the environment and effect these events had on the lives of those involved.

Any resemblance to actual persons, living or dead, events, concerns, businesses or locales is entirely confidential.

INTRODUCTION TO THE STRUGGLE

A breakthrough into the so called white market, was then seen as an opportunity of a life time. The apartheid regime realized with time that the economy of the country could no longer be sustained by the white man alone. The eighty/ twenty percent principle was no longer applicable (i.e.)whereby, twenty percent of the economically active citizens of the country could easily sustain the economy, whilst the eighty percent of the population contributed very little or none. This scenario was rife, whereby the non-white community were engaged in manual jobs and the white community were protected by law to occupy certain jobs under the job reservation act. The apartheid policy ensured that economical power was entrenched within its community, whilst the majority of the people were subjected to perpetual abject poverty and economical marginality. Over the years the pillars of the apartheid regime were gradually being eroded as some large business consortiums were struggling to make budgets. The jobs that were initially not available to the non-white community, were suddenly made available. Several companies started to advertise for sales people from the non-white community. The broad-casting co-operation needed educators to be involved in spearheading certain programs on television channels, designed specifically to communicate with the masses in their own mother tongue. Commercial banks opened their doors to the black masses, positions of bank-tellers, consultants and other prestigious positions were being occupied by blacks. Several more doors were being opened to the black masses, managerial positions were made available to the masses especially to those who had the required credentials. There were non-white pharmaceutical representatives who were employed by some pharmaceutical companies, these were mainly multi-national companies which had invested in South Africa. I was fortunate to be amongst those who penetrated the pharmaceutical market at that crucial time. Change was eminent, but a bit too slow as the masses were losing their patients. The pleasant odor of imminent freedom was already in the air, comments from the media was also in circulation, hence the lack of comprehension by the masses, as to the cause of delay.

The non-white clients needed to identify with people of their colour, working in the townships had become dangerous and risky for the white man, especially following the 1976 riots. This phenomenon also forced the apartheid regime to review some of its policies. The pillars of apartheid were gradually withering off, their relevance was becoming more and more questionable by the day. Change was inevitable, white faces in some institutions were being replaced by those of colour. The white community was struggling to accept the ***non-white*** persons in positions that were formally occupied by them. On the other hand the black masses had no previous experience nor work exposure, all they were bequeathed with, was their text book knowledge.

I can only relate what transpired within the pharmaceutical companies, as this is a more familiar territory. Those who were employed by the pharmaceutical companies experienced a real rough time, as their colleagues were hesitant to accept or even to recognize them. The hostility and the animosity that was displayed by some members of the white community was immense. By 1992, I could see more and more non-white representatives who entered the pharmaceutical industry, this was evident that the demise of the apartheid regime was inevitable.

Having been a medical representative for several years, working for different pharmaceutical companies, I was promoted to a senior position. This was when I really started to feel the harshness of the apartheid system. The managers, the personal assistants (s) they all behaved indifferently towards me. Some managers tried very hard to accommodate me. The worst were the day to day encounters, which I experienced with my immediate boss whom, I had to report to for several years. We often had these conflicting situations whereby our relationship would be so volatile, that sometimes I would be tempted to tender in my resignation.

I had never before thought of writing a book, but on this particular morning, I had just returned from one of the many confrontations with my immediate boss. I was trying very hard to overcome my anguish and resume with my work. I suddenly thought to myself, I needed to share my experience with someone out there. My confrontational encounters with my immediate boss had suddenly increased in their frequency, and the more they increased the more severe they became. The thought of sharing my story kept haunting me, political related questions became deterring factors. The desire was embraced by a friend of mine, who thought that it was a great idea.

The day arrived when I decided to put pen to paper, this proved to be a break-through for me, from then onwards things started to happen, I never looked back. I realized that I needed to gather lots of information, I was grateful that my mother was still alive because I depended on her for family history and other information from several other sources. My mother had this impeccable memory, she knew all our birth dates, all in all she was statistically orientated and she also kept a file with important documents. My baptismal certificate, my standard six certificate and my junior certificate were also with her, my matriculation certificate was safely kept with my other valuable documents in our home. I decided to create a file whereby I recorded all interactions and kept all the documents of each and every encounter I had with my boss and several other members of management.

I was progressing very well, but some haunting questions that frightened me, were; which publisher would risk his reputation by publishing this book? Was I now inviting the apartheid forces into our home?, Was I now going to stigmatize our family?. Was I now going to be labeled a "*TERRORIST*"?, I had to overcome my fears, because the desire to tell my story was equally challenging. Little did I know that the apartheid policies would be written off as a non-philosophical system by the stroke of a pen. Those white South Africans who made the rules that governed our country, were suddenly thrust into oblivion over night.

The government of national unity at the time, set aside time to formulate what is known as the constitution of the Republic of South Africa, 1996. Entrenched in the constitution is the 'freedom of expression', under the 'BILL OF RIGHTS', one of the corner stone of our democracy.

ACKNOWLEDGEMENT

This book is dedicated to my family, friends, my teachers from high school, my tutors in the nursing profession and university, my managers in the pharmaceutical industry.

My late father who instilled in me the many qualities, the demeanor that many a manager never ceased to challenge, unfortunately he would not be able to share this book with me, nor read the message of gratitude. He raised this girl to become a woman of stature, worth recognition. He taught me life as a whole, assisted me in developing a critical mind. Through politicizing my mind I developed assertiveness, accept myself for who I am—self identity.

My mother who put into perspective the nurse who had to stay focused. She had the most easy task, that was to put the cherry on top of the cake. She took up the responsibility by ensuring that my dreams, my philosophy and my goals in life were achieved. Each year for the past four years, whilst I was on training, I visited my home regularly, my mother would make sure that my stay was a memorable one.

My beloved husband who has been a supporting force behind me for all the years that I have been struggling to be myself and sustaining who I really am.

Mosholadi our eldest daughter who during trying times she would assume my role of being mother and eldest sister to her siblings.

Ntshwara-ngwako, our second daughter who is a replica of me, always strives to sustain her identity, she would insist on the life of this book in spite of all odds.

Matete, our eldest son, he is very computer literate, he was the steering figure behind the interpretation, the research, the phrasing and all other staff that is related to compilation of this book to its completion and finally it being dispatched.

Lephato, our youngest son, he is very good with the queen's language, expressive assertiveness were the theme through out, his perseverance and persuasiveness saw this book to its finality.

My friends whose friendship I value to this very day, those who were my study mates when we spent sleepless nights, burning the midnight oil, trying very hard to meet deadlines for submission of our assignments, I so much treasure these relationships that had been sustained for many, many years.

My apologies to my primary school teachers as I was too young to remember their names, however my sincere gratitude to them as they contributed in the primary socialization of Matema.

My high school teacher, I forgot his first name, except that the students called him Mr Majola he was the mathematics teacher.

My class teacher, Mr Mbiwa had been very supportive, he organized for me to write my final matriculation examination in another province.

The headmaster of the school, who ensured that we were channeled to the various institutions and colleges.

The members of the nursing profession who ensured that my training was smooth till completion.

The pharmaceutical companies that employed me, who assisted me to achieve one of my goals, according to Maslow's theory of needs, self-actualization.

An international university that assisted me in the work shop of the manuscript.

Regards

Matema Magagane

CHAPTER I

Background

This book is based on a true life story lived from day to day. Born in Pietersburg on the 27 October, 1942 to Rachel and Lotah Sehwana. My father moved from Pietersburg to Johannesburg and later moved to Cape Town, as many young men did during those days, they went out very early to try and find work in the big cities, far away from home. The trend during those days was that when this young man came to the big city, he would initially keep in contact with the family back home, but sooner the family would be forgotten. The most common employment in those days was in the mines, this type of work involved the digging of gold and diamonds underground. This category of labourers were known as migrant workers, who only went home periodically, (ie) when the mines closed during the festive season or during their annual leave.

The tendency was that these young men would establish relationships with the local people, they would have local wives and children, thus the family that was left behind in the rural areas was invariably forgotten.

In view of this scenario, we considered ourselves fortunate, in that my/ our father did remember to come back home to fetch his family, who comprised of my mother, my elder sister, brother and myself.

I am the second daughter in a family of five, three daughters and two sons. All five of us were educated in Cape Town in the so-called coloured schools.

I judged that, this was an influence from my father who was literate, he had passed his standard six before going to the second world war. Standard six then I presume was 'The Royal Readers' education system, presumably it was the British system of education, which he definitely knew was of a superior standard.

As a child I could recall, that under the bed in my parent's bedroom, there used to be a leather trunk, stuffed with former war veteran's attires (i.e.) amongst other things, a winter full-coat, a strong broad leather belt with a metal buckle, engraved with some initials, a copper helmet, a pair of large sized leather boots and some badges resembling those of foreign country's national flags.

I would somehow imagine this large structured, 6 foot (+/-2meter) tall, well builtman, fully dressed in this attire, presumably at war fighting for his beloved country.

I would have loved to treasure these, but truly I do not remember what really happened to them, what a loss!.

I passed my standard six with a first class with good symbols if there were any, but all it meant for me, was an entry to higher education.

In the later years, things became tough as the government at that time was in the process of dividing the rainbow nation of South Africa into different race groups who were categorized by the colour of one's skin. People were being uprooted and were forcibly being moved from their places of living to some unknown destination. The coloured and Indian communities were left behind to stay in the recently proclaimed residential area for coloured and Indian people. This process created so much havoc and pandemonium amongst the black people. Some families we knew had disappeared over night without a trace. The masses were then further divided into several ethnic groups and were being allocated houses according to their ethnic groups. These consisted of zones (eg) zone 1-5 would be allocated to the xhosa speaking people and the sotho speaking people would be allocated to stay in zone 6-10 etc. Some of the people rejected the process as they had ownership of their properties, those who did not have ownership were willing to be relocated, and the latter group was in the majority. There was also the group that consisted of others, this group neither owned a house nor property and had no permit to reside in Cape Town. The masses were then being moved from Athelone, Belgravia, Elsies River to Nyanga and Gugulethu and the group that consisted of others were sent back to Transkei or Lesotho. The government trucks were fully involved in transporting the people with their goods to the new residential areas, soon to be known as the locations or townships. (These areas were designed specifically to secure a perpetual supply of a labour force.)

These new areas consisted of small houses, each with three or four rooms per family. In my eyes they looked very orderly neatly arranged in rows, each row being demarcated by a gravel road, and only the main roads were tarred. These houses did not have electricity, however there were street lights and some homes were fortunate to share the street light at no extra cost. A single water-tap catered for several families and was placed between ten to twelve (10-12) houses. Transport into town was galore except that town had become very far and expensive. There were lots of playing grounds and some areas had tennis courts, grounds for basket-ball and large soccer or rugby fields.

There were three primary schools in our area, which meant that one had a choice, but by then I was ready for high school. The black masses in Cape Town consisted of 70% Xhosas, 25% Southern Sothos and a very small minority were a combination of Zulus, Northern Sothos, Vendas and other ethnic groups. The Xhosa speaking people dominated in this province, most of the schools taught isixhosa as a vernacular or first language and a few offered Southern Sotho or no other black language.

The government subsequently built more schools and these were once more divided according to the ethnic groups.

The education system that was taught in the schools, was the Bantu education which was designed to ensure that the black masses remained subservient to their masters. This system of education was definitely not one of the best, it yielded lesser numbers of scholars who achieved the Junior certificate and even fewer who matriculated, and only a hand-full who achieved tertiary or university qualifications.

On the other hand the average parent worked very hard to provide education for their children. As mentioned that these townships were situated far from the city, the average parent left home in the early hours of the morning and returned late in the evening from work in the city. This set-up caused immense strain on all parties (the children and the parents), the family fiber was gradually being eroded the price was untold.

There was a peculiar family staying in the neighbourhood, as a child I had never before seen this kind of set-up. The gentleman was one of my father's home boys, they were from the same village and they were both ex-war veterans.

He had returned from the war with a white woman, whom he had met in Europe and had married her and had brought her back home in his country.

The couple had three children, two girls and a boy, they lived on this isolated property far away from the rest of the community. As mentioned that he and my father were homeboys, they visited each other regularly and occasionally shared a drink. However what was strange to me, was that we yearned to play with their children, but that was never to be, until we parted ways during the time of the mass relocation. The children and their mother were always in doors except when their father would transport them to and back from school.

This property as mentioned was a bit far away from the rest of the other properties, it had a high wire fence right round with only two openings, one for pedestrians and the other for motor vehicles.

They had two large dogs, I did not know what breed they were, all I knew was that they resembled the police dogs.

They were quite vicious, and they were always chained, but they were allowed to run from one end of the gate to the other end on opposite sides. They ran along two separate thick wires that were embedded in the ground on either side, that also stretched from the one gate to the other separately.

I remember as children on our way to the shops, we enjoyed teasing these dogs by running very close to the fence, knowing very well that nothing would happen to us. In response these dogs would start barking frantically at us and simultaneously running along these wires, within the enclosed property. Later on in life I thought to myself that, this must have been very frustrating for them.

I had always wondered what could have happened to this family, and if they were relocated to one of the townships, I could have met or heard of them at some stage or another.

The most likely possibility, was that they could have been re-classified as coloured people, and were then left to reside on their property in Athelone, which had recently been proclaimed a residential area for the coloured/Indian community.

It was in 1952, I must have been in standard-one or two, we were told that the following day we were to dress-up in our full school uniform as the school was to expect very, very important visitors from overseas. We were also told that we were to sing one of our best songs for the guests. Our guests finally arrived, and our class was the one which was to present the guests with a song. We were on the stage and our guests were sitting in the front row facing the stage. As children, you can imagine that each one of us wanted to sing the loudest or the best in order to impress our guests. I always had this vivid memorable picture of this beautiful lady, who was standing at the end of the staircase and shook each and everyone's hand as we were getting off the stage, this was after we had sung our favourite song. This hand shake was indeed a memorable one, as each and everyone of us semi-bent our knees as we were extending our hands for the greeting. This is our culture whenever a younger person greets an older person, one would slightly bend both knees as a sign of respect. I had never before seen a white person at such close proximity, let alone a hand shake. That very afternoon when I got home I was still very excited and told my father what had happened at school, it was then that I learnt that, the beautiful lady was indeed the queen of England. I would not be mistaken, if I could recollect an event that happened some fifty-odd years ago, that during the very following year a large sized, one-penny, bronze coin was in circulation. On the flip side of the coin was the portrait of the beautiful lady who visited our school and shook my hand. "What a privilege and an honour!"

My younger sister was growing up very fast and was gradually looking more like my mother who was a pretty woman, I suppose in the eyes of every child one's mother is always seen as being the most beautiful person. People made comments such as my younger sister had better looks than mine. It did not take me long to realize that it was indeed true. I soon realized that this competition which was fast coming up between us, would eventually tear us apart.

I remember one day I was almost assaulted by my ex-boyfriend because I confronted him for proposing to my younger sister. Whenever I had a boyfriend our relationship would last for as long as my sister stayed out of the scene, but should it happen that she did show up, I automatically knew that I had lost him, but I would keep my cool so as to stay in control as an elder sister.

In those days the education department was structured in a very positive manner in that those pupils who performed well during their June (ie) half-yearly examinations, were being promoted to the next class. This meant that a bright student was not given the opportunity to idle, but his/her mind was kept challenged throughout his/her schooling. I happened to be amongst the few fortunate pupils who enjoyed this privilege especially at primary school.

My chances of being admitted in a coloured school were absolutely nil. I was then admitted to the local high School, where I started with standard seven, which was basically a repetition of standard six. This was the only high school in Cape Town which catered for thousands of black students. Subjects were grouped in a peculiar manner, I was forced to take up mathematics as a subject of which I was not particularly good at, but because the Southern Sotho class, which was the only one in the school, I had to be in this class. What was strange to me was the fact that I did very well in what was termed mental arithmetic, I recall achieving very high marks in arithmetic tests, but strangely I could not just cope with mathematics. This subject became a nightmare for me, however I managed to pass my Junior certificate (standard eight) in record time. This time it was an ordinary pass, but I did obtain good symbols as I was allowed to proceed to matriculation first year.

During those days the principal or headmaster of the school had the obligation to assist the government to channel students to only two professions (i.e.) teaching and nursing, unless the parents could afford for further education.

The school principal would then apply to the various institutions on behalf of the students, forms would be sent, filled in and be returned to the various institutions, they would then wait for the year-end results. I subsequently learned that a similar procedure was being followed in other high schools in the country as well.

My father had in the meantime opened up a small business, he had bought himself a van with a canopy which he used to collect offal (parts cut off as less valuable from carcass), meant for human consumption especially parts like the head, liver, intestines, heart, and kloutjies (limbs of carcass) from the abattoir in Somerset-west and sold these at a small profit. This business grew very well, my mother who was then working as a domestic, was asked to leave off her job to assist with the running of the business. Eventually the whole family was involved, except my elder sister and brother as they were in boarding school in Johannesburg. After school the three of us would join my parents and one of us would start delivering the nearby orders on foot, the customers appreciated this, as big concerns did not provide such services. Some orders were placed on a weekly or monthly basis, we had established a regular customer base. I in particular enjoyed adding up the debts and credits (i.e.) balancing of the books. I had an advantage over the others, in that I knew exactly who was owing how much, for what and when was the debt made. The menu for the ordinary man in the street were delicacies like fried liver, roasted heart and sometimes the head of the carcass, these consisted of the main course for Sundays and the rest of the offal (eg) intestines, lungs, stomach etc were menus for the rest of the week.

It so happened that one Saturday afternoon I was on a debt collecting spree, carrying the debtor's book, my sister insisted on accompanying me, I did not really enjoy anyone's company, especially when I was dealing with the so-called chronic or long standing debtors, as I had developed an antagonistic approach, only known by me.

The very first house that we went to had three dogs, two small ones and a medium sized one, I would not say they were vicious dogs, but they would attack their victim in such a manner that instilled fear into one causing one to flee and they would automatically give chase.

I usually carried a stick to handle these dogs, but on this particular day I forgot about protecting ourselves. I watched them as they came charging at us, initially I thought I could handle the situation, somehow we were overwhelmed, we panicked and started running away, as we were running away, for some reason, they were all after my sister and because they were biting her ankles and tearing pieces from her dress, she was screaming from the pain. I then decided to pick up a few stones which I threw at the dogs, and it was only then that they retreated, but the harm was already done.

I was just as upset and above all I was concerned about my father's reaction, I really did not expect a hiding and to my surprise I got a good one for that matter.

Thinking back to my school holidays, I used to enjoy helping my mother in her job as a domestic, that was before she was asked to leave off to assist my father with the running of the business. During this time I had learnt to prepare several dishes especially delicacies for the English speaking families. I could also do a few odd jobs like cleaning of silver cutlery, and washing and ironing as there were no washing machines in those days, window cleaning, scrubbing and floor polishing, all these were done manually. This was a regular routine as mentioned, I looked forward to the school holidays, as I had set simple goals for myself, like buying myself vanishing face cream, lip-ice, some perfumes, body lotions and other necessities which I knew that my father could not afford, let alone giving us pocket money.

I saw this new business as something which was going to interfere with my objectives, not that I did not enjoy being of assistance to my parents and also I could clearly see the way forward as there was more disposable income for us as a family. My mother who knew my needs had in the meantime secured my occupation during school holidays with a friend called Ausi-Hilda. My first impression of Ausi-Hida's madam was not a good one, she was not interested to know my name, but decided to nickname me pikinini. (a derogative name for a black child) I soon discovered that Ausi-Hilda's employers were not the best of families, the so-called madam of the house would often scream at Ausi-Hilda in my presence, sometimes we would share a plate of food, in-spite of me having to do the extra jobs like, cleaning windows, washing curtains for the whole house and several other jobs, her credibility in my eyes was being gravely tarnished with each encounter.

It was one morning as Ausi-Hilda was preparing breakfast for the family, she accidently broke a cup, which she had to replace, in my eyes, that was being most inconsiderate. I did not know how much Ausi-Hilda was earning, but all I knew was that when it was time for me to go back home to prepare for school re-opening, she would give me a few shillings from her own pocket, this too broke my heart, but I was not keen to upset her by turning down the offer.

There was one thing I learned from this experience, was the fact that I must never ever in my lifetime, find myself in a similar situation, that was to be employed as a domestic servant or a maid as commonly referred to by their madams during their conversations, each one talking proudly about her maid as if they owned this commodity, and for me to ensure that I lived up to my commitment, I needed to be educated. When I looked back to my mother's ex-employers, I realized that they were a far better family, they had also set high standards in my mind. I recall that the lady of the house used to take the opportunity herself to thank me, she would offer me a few shillings herself, and she would encourage me to study hard. The lady of the house was a primary school teacher, who stayed with her aged mother in a very large house. This also seemed strange to me, only two persons staying in such a large house, I asked myself, questions like, was it possible for these two persons to occupy or just to walk into each room everyday of their lives? and if so, when?, which was very unlikely, so, why not offer my family a few rooms?. What actually struck me was the fact that my family was a much larger family than my mother's employer and yet we were squashed in a little three roomed house and were expected to live happily ever after.

As mentioned my father was literate, he used to read the local newspapers, copies of the government gazette and would interpret the contents to us, he gently politicized us, especially me. I had this questioning mind I always asked what people termed silly questions (identity document for blacks only) Why would you show your dompas to this little white boy?", whom I judged to be illiterate. Somehow I had an opportunity to prove my point. I soon discovered that they only received minimal education and they knew only one language and that was their mother tongue, other languages were foreign to them. When confronted they would try by all means to inform me in no uncertain terms that sooner or later they would be chasing me and locking me up for the very same offence, *failure to produce my dompas*, which should be on my body 24/7 (ie) for twenty four hours a day and for seven days a week. Wow what a mammoth task?

This would infuriate me, that I would answer back very rudely, and in response they would shout back at me "houjoubekjong".(shut-up). Then it did not make much sense to me, until one evening after my father had read the local newspaper then *The Cape Atlanta*, that he told us that a clause in the statutory books of the country pertaining to that effect was underway. Non-European women from the age of eighteen years (Non-European women, a term used to describe black women) were to carry a dompas.

The government of the day spent millions of pounds for this kind of service, whereby fully fledged policemen drove around the townships, stopping people at random, demanding for this dompas, and failure to produce constituted to commitment of a crime. People preferred to stay indoors, rather than to risk spending a night in jail. Socializing with friends or relatives was minimal as the majority of the people did not own motor vehicles, and any socialization would be done on foot, thus exposing one to unnecessary imprisonment.

This dompas was supposed to serve as an identity document designed to assist the bearer and the employer in an agreement in terms of the employment contract, instead it was being used in the most antagonistic and inhumane manner to the black people only. The thought that I would soon be carrying a dompas, made me feel helpless, angry and subjugated.

As a young girl growing up in the township, several things that happened in our community used to leave me with plenty of unanswered questions. I used to watch in amazement how the large companies would come around to repossess goods especially furniture from homes in the neighbourhood, this was a regular process especially during the first three-six months of the year. A brief explanation, the working class, the black majority worked for companies whereby they would be offered a thirteenth cheque, sometimes called 'bonus', this consisted of an extra month's/week's salary offered only in December, which was meant for Christmas shopping. This money would instead be used to pay a deposit towards the much desired furniture, with very little consideration nor planning as to how the installments were to be sustained during the following months or years. There was not much money going around in our community in those days, our houses we rented as no black person was allowed to own property nor land in the urban areas, which were proclaimed white areas. Having spent Christmas and new-year in a well furnished, beautiful house, the furniture companies would come around to collect their furniture as the people were in arrears for three to six months. The hurt and pain endured by the women during this process (the actual repossession of the goods) was insurmountable, and what was evident, was the manner in which they cried and screamed for help.

This process really broke my heart, and in my mind, there was only one beneficiary, the furniture company.

Things were progressing very well at my home, everybody knew his or her responsibility, we had established a routine in terms of our individual roles, all in all life was running smoothly for the Sehwana family. Gone were the days when we each had only one pair of shoes which we wore to school and on Sundays, these shoes would be worn strictly for going to school and back, and on Sundays we were allowed to wear them to church and back, the rest of the time we were on bare foot. To this day my clothes that I wear on Sundays are different from my clothes that I wear when going to work, call it indoctrination or just a habit that one cannot get rid-of.

Sometimes I would accompany my father to the abattoir and watch him, with so much admiration, when he would be doing business with the white-man, I must say these interactions and transactions created indelible memories in my mind.

On some other days, when there would be lots of offal leftover, and because we did not have a large refrigerator, my father and I would then drive around in the township to try and sell the remaining offal.

I used to enjoy these special trips as they happened very seldom, we would stop at some café to buy fish and chips, some kit-gat bread and some cold-drinks which I ate with much eagerness.

The business had grown financially, there was obviously a lot more disposable income, this was evident specially during Christmas, my father would provide my mother with sufficient money for shopping. I would not say that my mother bought from expensive shops, but all I appreciated were the beautiful dresses we wore on Christmas day. Sometimes when there would be some money remaining my mother would then buy an extra attire for each one of us to wear on New year's day. This was regarded as sheer luxury, because the norm was that the attire which was worn on Christmas day would be worn again on New year's day.

During June holidays I received a letter from the matron at Phuthaditjaba Hospital, who briefly informed me that as soon as I turned eighteen (18) years I would be admitted for training asa student nurse. This letter did not mean much to me then, as I was looking forward to completing matriculation and I also had a few other plans rolled up my sleeve. A few years later my father became ill, he suffered a severe stroke and was admitted to Kgatelo-pele Hospital. He was then released a few weeks later, I was very disturbed to realize that he could not use his right arm and leg, he had suffered a stroke that left him with a right sided paralysis and he was also speechless. The doctors had given my mother strict instructions to prepare a salt-free diet for my father, he had to be taken out of bed every morning and made to sit on an armchair in the veranda. All these happenings had disrupted our family routine, my father could no longer drive to Somerset-west abattoir, the business was in danger of closing down, I could drive but I was not licensed to drive on a public road. During this time we were all under a lot of stress, I had to wake up much earlier to assist my mother in nursing my father. My mother would wash him, dress him up and I would assist her to carry him to the armchair in the veranda. I failed to comprehend as to how could such a strong, well built, healthy man suddenly become so helpless and dependent on my mother for everything (e.g.) washing, clothing, feeding etc.

Life had changed drastically especially for me per se, my elder sister and brother were called during this time and they had returned to Johannesburg to their respective jobs and try to help support the family. I could no longer cope with my school work, each day seemed much longer, I could foresee my plans being thwarted. I could no longer think straight, in the meantime my mother had to return to her former employer in order for us to survive.

Correspondence between us and my elder sister and brother never ceased, in one of the letters, my sister had suggested that I leave school to find work, this upset me very much, to console me she re-phrased her words by advising me, that at least I had obtained a Junior Certificate (standard eight) and this was a requirement for admission to the nursing profession. I thought of the letter that I had received from the matron of Phuthaditjaba Hospital sometime ago. I had to swallow my pride and initiate for correspondence to resume. It did not take long for the matron to respond and what was most exciting, was the fact that I could start training as a student-nurse on the first of November the same year. When I broke the news to my class-teacher he was very upset, as he was in the process of assisting me with my school work, for the very first time I confided in him and told him that this was the only option available.

However my teacher offered what he thought was best, by ensuring that I wrote my final matriculation in one of the schools in Johannesburg. I realized later what pains he endured to arrange with the matrons and the Bantu Education Department to ensure that I did indeed write my final examinations. My father passed on a few months before I left for Johannesburg to resume training as a student-nurse in one of the largest hospitals in the southern hemisphere.

This was one of the saddest moments in my life, I was emotionally bruised. My father was my icon, my role model, my pillar of strength and someone I had always looked up to, he had instilled in me a lot of good qualities, that I endear and practice to this day.

My world had suddenly crumbled right from underneath my feet, I thought to myself that he had died too soon, he had just turned sixty-one (61) years. I recall on some of our business trips we would discuss various topics and one of his dreams, he shared with me, would be for him to see us as professional people someday, and yet death robbed him of this lifetime opportunity.

I only had my mother to lean onto and I soon discovered that she was indeed a strong woman and with her beside me I had to decide to wipe away my tears, be strong and face life head on. My mother provided me with all the necessities that were required for my training, things like brown laced-up shoes, a pair of scissors, a watch with a second hand (this was for counting the pulse), an iron and she bought me a few other things that I came to appreciate later. She was also very happy for me, because she knew that I was a determined young lady, who could adjust to any situation.

CHAPTER II

Life in the big city

Arrangements were made for my departure to the big city, bidding my friends farewell was not easy, but I had to do it. My mother had also bought me some new clothes and a few necessities that later became very useful.

I started training on the first November and I completed three and a half years later. This was not a smooth path, sometimes it was very thorny and up heal, however with the support of the senior professionals, I did manage to reach the end of the road. Conditions of training were that after completion, six months were spent serving a contract before being registered as a qualified, professional nurse with the professional body in the country governing the practice of nursing as a profession.

Whenever any young person especially a girl is about to leave her/his hometown for the big city, one would be given a lecture on all the bad things that happened in the big city. Strange stories that happened to other people were common things that were told over and over. I took these warnings very serious, in order for me to ensure my safety, I made sure that I only travelled by bus and rarely by taxi. On my day-off I would go shopping with a friend in the city, sometimes we would go watch a movie in Fordsburg or we would visit my friend's family as she was a local girl. These trips were kept to a minimum. Sometimes I would visit my elder sister who lived in one of the townships in Soweto, I would enjoy the day with her family, but I would make sure that by sunset I was in the nurses home, (living-in quarters within hospital premises) One may call it phobia of the unknown, but I was always mindful of any potential harm or danger.

Something that I really appreciated in this part of the world, was that my home language was spoken by most of the people, occasionally one would meet some-one who spoke isiZulu or any other language. This was in the Transvaal where Sotho speaking people were in large numbers and dominated the region.

One afternoon as I was returning from a visit from my sister's place, a young man boarded the same bus and decided to sit next to me, the driver of the bus who happened to be my relative introduced me to this young man. Remember that I grew up in Cape Town, we knew no relatives of ours and we were always told that most of our relatives were in Transvaal or Johannesburg, so this bus driver was one of my many relatives.

The young man seemed very friendly and pleasant and we started chatting, and I was still mindful of strangers.

Two weeks later I was surprised to be called and told that I had a visitor, and guess who? that young-man!, I was taken aback, I thought to myself, something I said or did must have impressed him, for him to take the trouble to pay me a visit. I had forgotten his name and this was quite embarrassing, however what was evident was the fact that he wanted to know me better. We could not chat much, because I was still on duty and I did not want to be seen as someone irresponsible. I then decided to dismiss him as quickly as I could, he insisted on enquiring about my next day-off, which I told him. On my day-off, I was again called from my room by a colleague who informed me that I had a visitor. I was expecting him but not so early, I still remember, the time was 10h30, and on my day-off, supposedly my resting day, of which I preferred to sleep until late.

We sat in the nurses guest room, I did not know what we were going to chat about, however we did chat about something, by the time we parted he had secured a date for our next appointment. We soon started dating and I did not find much time for introspection in-between our appointments, but all I knew was that, I looked forward to seeing him on each and every date. During our conversations, we discovered that we had quite a few things in common (e.g.) our parents were both from Pietersburg, which meant that we shared the vernacular language, our uncles were both ministers of religion, though different denominations and we also shared a few hobbies. Surprisingly this particular stranger was getting very close to my heart. We had become an item, we spent most of our free time enjoying each other's company. Whenever this young man visited me, he would bring me a bouquet of fresh roses, or a large slab of chocolate, I was very impressed as I had never been treated in this manner before. To sum it up he had become my best friend. I had never thought that I could enjoy some one's company ever again since my father's passing on, and yet here was someone who walked into my life and captured my heart.

Time had come for me to make a decision, and I thought of introducing him to my family, I was indirectly seeking their approval. Three and a half years had passed on very quickly and our training was nearing its end. This was a crucial time, decisions were to be made pertaining to one's future and my future, I had decided, laid with this young-man, who had become a part of me. I could not imagine life without him.

The day arrived when the much awaited question was asked, which was "would you spend the rest of your life with me?", to which I excitedly answered, "Yes".

The customary requirements (lobola) money paid by the bridegroom to the parents of the bride were fulfilled, the two families negotiated for the dates for the actual celebrations, whereby a cow would be slaughtered for the occasion. We could not afford an engagement party, however we did utilize the same evening after the customary celebrations to announce our engagement.

My wedding day was another memorable occasion in my life. My whole family, relatives and friends were present to witness the occasion and to offer their support for me.

This was a well organized wedding celebration. My uncle escorted me to church and handed me over to my husband to be (in a few moment's time) as he stood patiently waiting near the alter, in anticipation for the very same moment. After celebrating the matrimonial part of the wedding, which took place in a Catholic church, we sped-off to have photos taken and we then returned to share a splendid lunch with our guests. The remaining part of the later afternoon was utilized by the family elders who were advising us, the (newlyweds) as to how to share our lives together as man and wife.

We were given presents in many forms, some were material things others were vouchers and hard cash money, all these were highly appreciated as they gave us a good start for our home. We could not afford a honeymoon, however we did manage to spend a few days together at his uncles place in Pietersburg, before returning to our respective jobs.

The journey had started, this was the beginning of our life together, Wow, how exciting!

I always had this guilt feeling at the back of my mind, which later came to the fore, that I had married too soon, I should have ploughed something back to my family. I felt like I owed them, occasionally I would dismiss this guilt feeling by trying to justify it, by reassuring myself, that I had never disappointed, or disgraced my family in anyway. This guilt feeling haunted me for some time and I was on the look-out for any potential opportunity.

Several years later, I saw this opportunity, my nephew had passed his matriculation examination, obtaining very good symbols and his parents could not afford tertiary education, so I took it upon myself to sponsor him, hopefully I would later find some peace in my mind.

We had initially planned for the wedding to take place after completing my training, and that was shortly after serving my contract. We had also planned to raise a family before involving ourselves in large debts. I became pregnant the following year and I then stayed home for two years, raising our eldest daughter. Two years later we were again blessed with our second daughter and we were later blessed with two sons, and within the period of eight years, we had become a jolly good family of six. Raising four young children was a bit heavy, and by this time I had felt the strain of my chosen profession, because I had to return to work in between confinements. Each confinement on average lasted one to two years, and maternity benefits were limited during those days.

During this time the South African governing body for the practice of nursing had recently opened up opportunities for nurses to improve their academic qualifications. This opportunity came at the right time as there was so much stagnation within the profession. I saw this avenue as an ideal opportunity to develop myself and the only option I had, was to study privately with an internationally recognized University.

As mentioned the strain was having a negative effect on me, Phuthaditjaba Hospital being the largest hospital in the Southern hemisphere, rendered services to patients from local townships, the reef, the outskirts in the surrounding areas and the neighbouring states, this meant real hard work.

An incident that I feel compelled to share whilst I was nursing during the Soweto riots, I had never in my time of practice as a nurse witnessed anything like this. I found myself caught up in the middle of a catastrophe, and according to my oath, mine was to preserve life at all times. I was working in casualty at the time, when we were admitting children in large numbers who had gun-shot wounds, they were crying and screaming as they endured the severity of the pains. There was blood all over, the staff was over whelmed with the amount of work, we could no longer cope, more staff was brought in from the wards to assist. As the day progressed we worked ourselves to the bone, there was no tea or lunch break and the injured children continued to be brought in by ambulances and some by private cars.

We soon heard that riots had erupted because there was confrontation between these children and the police. The townships had turned into a war zone, it was the police against the children, this continued for several days. The country was in total turmoil as the riots were spreading to the other townships around the country. Structures that were erected by the government were set alight, schools, government offices, beer-halls, libraries and all other structures that resembled white domination were destroyed. The attention was also directed to those who were suspected of being sell-outs by destroying their cars and homes, some police members were forced to leave their homes for fear of victimization.

The hospital was in a crisis, I suppose this was one of the first since world war two. We continued to work for several days and nights without going home to our families. We shared the shifts, whilst others went to rest others stayed on, but the hours we worked exceeded the normal working hours by far.

In between we would share meals and freshening up, which was mainly done at the nurses quarters.

During this time a lot of sacrifices were made and a lot of tears were shed as these were our children from our own communities.

It shook the nation to watch fully fledged soldiers, who were trained to protect the citizens of the country, who were now shooting and killing the very citizens they sought to protect, all in the name of self-defense?, self-defense against stone throwing children?.

What concerned me was, how those humble black South Africans had suddenly become aggressive, full of hatred, so destructive and thirsty for revenge. How the township blew up in flames in front of our eyes and as parents we could do nothing.

I could recall that shortly, prior to the riots, there was an article about the introduction of Afrikaans as the medium of instruction in the black schools and that several leaders in the community were preparing to handle the situation.

Over the years we, the society were subtly and carefully trained, that certain issues or grievances were best left to the specific or concerned people, hence this issue was left to the educators and the community leaders to sort out and least did we think that the children would take it upon themselves.

These soldiers would walk into casualty and demand that we hand over the injured children to them, because they considered them to be law-offenders who should be in jail.

These children were our patients and ours was to protect them as best as we could. Invariably we encountered some altercations with the police and they would report us to the hospital authorities and if things were to be done their way, these children should be handed over to them having received minimal medical treatment. They forgot one important fact, that these were our children and we were all from the same community, *the oppressed masses.*

The situation had become so volatile that a third force came into being and this aggravated the situation in the townships.

There was the other element which consisted of non workers they took over from the children and the whole objective was lost in the interim, as they continued to cause havoc in the townships by looting stores and committing other devious crimes.

They destroyed the homes of those people whom they suspected of being sellouts/informers/spies (terms used to label those who worked secretly for the government). Initially all structures that were representative of the government were being destroyed, and the situation had become uncontrollable, even those homes that belonged to the civil servants and some leaders in the community were also destroyed. There was total pandemonium in the townships all over the country.

Taking a walk in the evening was done at your own risk for fear of being a victim of any of these unruly elements.

Parents watched helplessly as their children disappeared into the neighbouring states, some into graves and some to this day, their where about still remain a mystery.

The aftermath of the riots remained with us, week-ends were no longer utilized to spend with the family, but we were now fully involved in burying our children one after the other, as they were overcome by complications which arose from the gun-shot wounds.

During this time the media kept the masses and the world informed of the riots as they progressed in the country, and suddenly this phenomenon changed, only selective information was announced on the media.

The government suddenly became aware of the potential harm that might be caused by these riots. However the news were already known worldwide that the country was experiencing a political crisis, (e.g.) the picture of the first victim, a thirteen year old pupil, who was being carried by another student, with the victim's sister running alongside, was seen all over the world.

When the dust had settled and the riots had ended, several lives were lost, what a waste of young lives, what a pity, what a shame!

These riots which went down in the books of history as June-16, marked the end of Christmas shopping for our children, there was no longer a need to celebrate Christmas day, thus the term *black Christmas*.

The masses had suddenly become conscious of their virtues in terms of their role in the economy of the country, which when interpreted in the layman's terms, one of them was their 'buying power', of which they now possessed full control.

These riots had negative effects on the economy of the country, the masses had abruptly ceased in their lavish way of spending especially during Christmas. This was the shop owner's time to make profit as they charged exorbitant prices for their goods

Typical of a divided nation, between those who do have and those who do not have, the former was not involved in the riots and later made comments in the newspaper, that they failed to understand the reason for these riots, because the government was funding for their (the latter) children's education, and what was the fuss all about?

The repercussions there of, had negative effects on the economy of the country, the masses had abruptly ceased in their lavish way of spending especially during Christmas. This was the shop owner's time to make large profits as they charged exorbitant prices for their goods.

The international markets saw us as a high risk country and was reluctant to engage us in their businesses. These riots reflected our country as being very unstable and not a suitable trading partner, all these bore negative repercussions, very little or no new investments or major deals came through. The country silently endured negative growths in most of the markets for some time.

Some months later a report by the commissioner enquiring into the riots, some of the information released in the news paper revealed that most of those children who had sustained gun-shot wounds at the back of their bodies, were shot at from behind, which meant that as the confrontation got heated up, the children must have panicked, got frightened and were shot at as they were turning to flee.

Several years later the black masses of the country were still in mourning, parents missed watching their little sons and daughters, who would have been dressed up in little elegant suits, and beautiful, colourful dresses in celebration of Christmas day, that was to be *no more*.

As mentioned earlier on, my chosen profession had become a thorn in my eye, I constantly thought about my pledge that I had made some years back, and the question which was equally daunting 'was it relevant in this day'?.

The working hours were stretched, night duty rotated even quicker than before, (i.e.) three months night duty to be served by each professional trained nursing sister per annum according to the conditions of employment, this condition was being violated by the employer. The workload had increased over the years and had by far out-numbered the nurse patient ratio in the rendering of total patient care. This was when I decided that time has come for me to surrender my noble profession, for a much lighter job, more pay, less stressful and spending

23

more time with my children, and this adventure was termed "seeking greener pastures."

When I first announced this to my husband and family they thought I had lost my mind. Their facts, when put on a scale, out-weighed my reasons for wanting to leave, words like in nursing there was security, chances of being promoted to higher ranks within the profession were pretty high, more so I had completed my degree.

All these facts I had done an intense monologue for several months and each time I reached the very same conclusion. My mother who knew me better than anybody else, told them to let go, even when she herself was not at the least impressed.

However there was no turning back, my children needed me especially our eldest daughter who was fast approaching her adolescence. I thought back of the few week-ends that I did spend with them, the question that always arose was "Mama why don't you cook nice food for us on Sundays and spend the day with us like other mums?". My thoughts went back to the days when a week-end off-duty was seen as a real treat and it was offered once a month per staff member and a month's leave once a year except December months.

Week-ends are days when everybody is home with their families, especially the children who needed to see their mother home, play games with them, help them with their school work and basically be there for them.

The houses which were provided by the government were very small, sometimes called *match boxes*, and if one needed a bigger house, this meant digging dipper into one's pocket. These were some of the necessities that we could not afford, our little family consisted of sons and daughters and needless to say they needed some privacy. In view of these unmet needs the desire for change was even greater.

I often reminisce about those days whilst I was working in the medical wards, I had always admired those ladies who regularly came to see heads of departments, the professors, the consultants and some of the doctors. I soon learnt that they were medical representatives working for different pharmaceutical companies and they were promoting products for their respective companies. Above all, besides looking smart, they had those pleasant looking faces, not stress laden, nor a frustrated facial appearance, this kind of scenario was a common sight in this hospital. This made me review my situation, I was in my mid thirties, quite slim and reasonably attractive, would this mean that in the next ten years, I'll be overweight, with my ankles drooping over my shoes and with my face which by then probably was already showing some signs of stress and frustration. With this bit of introspection, I became even more determined.

The agencies which were available were not placing black medical representatives and some were not brave enough to inform one. The search had started and this was a real bumping ride, I also realized that selling experience and a pharmaceutical background were prime requirements for this position.

The situation in South Africa was very different then, when a job was being advertised, the prospective company would specify whether a black, coloured or a white person was required. In some instances whereby the company was not specific, but as soon as they realized that the applicant was black, they would either inform the applicant that the position was reserved for a white person or they would simply asked if you were fully bilingual, this was another way of saying *no to the black masses*. Being fully bilingual meant that one should be able to speak and write in English and Afrikaans and the latter was a rare achievement with the black community. There was also the job reservation law enacted in the statutory books, that certain jobs were reserved for the white community only, whilst certain types of jobs were available for black people in spite of their level of education. Once more the black masses were relegated to being *hewers of wood and drawers of water*.

Most of my colleagues whom I graduated with, had left the country in search of greener pastures overseas. Recruitment agencies from the big cities abroad were interested in highly qualified nurses and recruited them in their thousands. This was what the media termed *brain drain* for South Africa.

Matema Magagane

Indeed this was a brain drain, because training nurses involved costs which were largely incurred by the South African government, whilst foreign countries enjoyed the benefits or the fruits there of.

The sad part to this exodus was that the patient, the tax payer, the citizen of the country received minimal health care.

I finally struck a job with a company as a Hygiene Consultant. My job entailed promotion of my company's products in the black schools, by educating the high school students on how to take care of their bodies during the changing phases in their lives. This consisted of a presentation on puberty, the physiological changes that their bodies undergo during this period and how to handle these, and finally this would grant me a platform to promote my company's products. The products were; sanitary pads, an antiseptic solution, roll-ons, toilet soaps, tooth pastes, skin lotion and super-c sweets. A sample of each product would be given to each student, depending on the gender, (e.g) the girls would be given everything else and in addition a starter pack of sanitary pads.

I enjoyed this job, my clients were school pupils and obtaining permission from the then department of Bantu Education was no problem, even the school principal saw this as an opportunity for the pupils to be taught about puberty by an outsider. Teaching adolescents about puberty used to be the responsibility of the parent or relative (e.g. the aunt) but with the changing times this responsibility was shunned and the school teacher resumed this role as there was a need to educate and make them aware of the dangers of having sex at an early age. The teachers could no longer cope, due to the work load. This responsibility was once more neglected and was later taken up by the nurses during their promotion campaign for the use of contraceptives.

I fitted in very well into this position, fulfilling a dual role, that of the parent and that of the advisor/nurse and simultaneously promoting my company's products, all parties were benefitting. Make no mistake I was very much aware of the situation of being exploited by the white supremacy, but then I needed the exposure into the so called sophisticated market. The remuneration was not bad, but definitely better and I also had a company car at my disposal, which I could use to take my kids to school, but unfortunately I could not fetch them after school as at that time I was still busy working. Our services were being appreciated, some schools would request a repeat presentation, as a result we could no longer cope with the demands. In the meantime our managers had seen the need to expand into other provinces as well, thus two more ladies were employed, one lady for each province (i.e.) Cape Town/ Western Cape and Durban/KwaZuluNatal. The company was doing well, for our national sales conference, we spent ten days at Durban in a posh hotel, all meals and drinks were provided at company costs.

Life had changed for the better for me, for my family and my children, who could invite me to attend parent's meetings and any other activities that took place in the evening. I came to realize that the company was indeed a small company, which was outsourcing from giant companies, contracts were signed and x-amount budgets were set to be achieved by end of the year, which were achievable, and that we were the first ladies to be employed, we were actually part of an expedition. This company consisted of three managers, two of them were directly involved with us and the other partner was involved with promotions in supermarkets, dealing with food stuff. We had a manager whom we reported to once a week and whenever a need arose. I soon realized that the manager was not well educated nor intelligent, his attitude and behaviour reminded me of the South African police force, their hostile attitude towards black people, to this day I still wander if he was not recruited from the police force. The manner in which he addressed us was appalling to say the least. My other colleagues were nurses and teachers by profession and they were all hard workers, but they would not dare challenge any verbal abuse from our manager, so I was eventually seen as the bad girl or *cheekygirl*, a term commonly used in the work place to denote someone who challenged the manager's authority. Somehow our manager became wise, by befriending me, I suspect that he must have noted that, I had become the hot favourite in the team, because whenever the giant companies who were potential or current clients who wished to see what we were doing, how we sold the products, the directors would ask me to represent the company and I would make sure that I did an excellent job. I knew that this meant more business for the company and somehow that they were a lot more dependent on these giant companies and of course my performance. I still recall one afternoon, having given a presentation to one of the prospective giant companies, one of the directors secretly gave me his business card and asked me to contact him as soon as possible, I surely did, but to my surprise he offered me a job, with a better car, better salary, bursaries for my children, initially I was taken up, but when I discussed this with my husband, he made me realize that I would be shooting myself in the foot, and the fact was that I had been in this market for less than a year and this would not reflect well on my c.v. (curriculum vitae)

It was one afternoon we were summoned to the office, one of the ladies working in Johannesburg had her car broken into, all her samples and personal belongings were stolen and she had reported the matter to the police. The hotel refused to take responsibility claiming that the 'car was parked at owners risk'. Our manager was very upset with her, he was actually blaming her, and that the cost of the stolen goods would be deducted from her remuneration. I expected her to object, and when she did not, so I took it upon myself to defend her, I also thought that all of us will at some stage or another, also become victims of a similar situation and once we accepted this set-up, there would be no turning back. I challenged the manager who was taken aback, he said something nonsensical, like "you keep quiet because you are not involved". I told him in no uncertain terms that should one of us be dismissed, we were all prepared to hand in our resignations. I knew that the company could not afford this, but within myself I was not too sure of the latter and above all could I afford this sacrifice?, and finally I asked for the director's view on the matter at hand. I also knew that the company would fold up and the directors would do anything to try and save the situation.

I loved this job, it was my very, very first exposure to the so-called white market, this was an opportunity of a life time.

I could feel the success within me, especially when we had giant companies contracting in, I looked forward to growing within and with this company. The directors enjoyed chatting with me and they would often ask me about my job and my stay within the company. Somehow I knew that they were testing my intelligence to assess whether, I knew my strengths or my potential. Invariably I would take this opportunity to express my gratitude and I would also in passing, throw in a few comments like, "how about having a black manageress?" no comments, issue not open for discussion, they had never heard of a black manager in those days, let alone a black manageress.

I worked for this company for two and half years and I realized that there were no opportunities for staff development, all that mattered was, sales figures, profits and budgets etc.

The company had grown and was still growing, accessibility to the directors was restricted, we only saw them during meetings or per appointment. I decided to enroll for a marketing diploma with a private Institution locally and I simultaneously placed my c.v. in the market place, this was another era of job hunting.

I was confident that I would strike a job of my choice, judging by my credentials that were recently added to my c.v. (curriculum vitae) the experience (art of selling). There was no advertisement that went by without a thorough screening and invariably I went through the same procedures again and again.

At last there was an advertisement in the local newspaper by a pharmaceutical company which required a medical representative to work in the so-called black areas. I contacted the company and an interview day was set. The interview was very interesting, out of fifteen applicants the list was reduced to five applicants, and we ended up being only two ladies. The final day arrived when the marketing director had to select one person for the position, and this person happened to be me. The night prior the interview, I had prepared myself very well, I had prepared answers to commonly asked questions (e.g.) What are your reasons for wanting to leave your present job?, I knew I had to be positive. I also prepared my physical appearance (e.g.) my hairstyle, my dress code, my makeup, though I don't really wear much, but special precautions were taken.

I had done my best to outshine my opponent. I resumed work on the first day of the month (October).

CHAPTER III

The real challenge

I underwent training for six weeks, this consisted of basic anatomy and physiology, a few days were spent on the company's products and a few hours were spent on selling skills. This was an American company with a branch based in South Africa in an industrial area, I happened to be the first black representative to be employed in this company. The staff behaved very differently, some could not even say Hi!, some ignored me, pretended that I didn't exist, whilst others were very friendly and were willing to show me around and how things were done in this company. As mentioned this was a multinational company, things were done methodically and meticulously. I soon found my way around, selling would always be selling except that I was selling to a different category of clients. My dress code and etiquette and style had to be different in order to depict my company's image, unlike my previous company we were provided with uniforms. I had to refurnish my wardrobe with real smart, classy and stylish out-fits. I was started off on a very good salary, which to me was a dream come true. I was bought one of the latest cars in the motoring industry as a company car, two of our children who were in high school were sponsored. All these benefits seemed unreal, until I heard about the Sullivan Code, signed in the United States of America by large black owned enterprises. These American conglomerates had agreed upon a code of social responsibility with all American companies that invested in the African countries to take responsibility to provide for the development of the indigenous people of Africa. Medical-aid was provided for my immediate family, money that I spent on refurnishing my wardrobe, I was allowed to claim from the taxman. All these benefits encouraged me to work even harder. There were also prizes commonly labeled by the representatives as *dangling carrots* which were being used to try and entice them to work hard, but I saw this as a real challenge.

Each representative had a budget to achieve by year-end. Our areas of work were divided by regions, then further into cities and towns and finally by a time-frame of six weeks to be spent in each area per representative. Five weeks were to be spent locally and one week outside the designated areas, which were known as country trips. My country trip was Lesotho and Swaziland, I soon did away with Lesotho due to the country's financial constraints. As much as this was an American company based in South Africa, it was managed by white South Africans and therefore apartheid rules applied. I was not allowed to work in the so-called white areas, so I had to obtain all my business in the so-called black areas.

I worked mainly in the townships, Indian and coloured areas. My main duties were to promote my products to pharmacies, wholesalers and private practitioners, also known as the general practitioner or the dispensing doctors. In some cases I would take direct orders and accompanied by payments and the wholesalers would do the deliveries, except in some urgent cases.

The company had excellent products which were a bit pricey for the average man in the street. The general practitioner also known as the dispensing doctor operated mainly in the townships, coloured and Indian residential areas.

A visit to the general practitioner proved to be a bit expensive, as mentioned that there was not much money in circulation in these communities.

The general practitioner had constructed a package, commonly known as the *flat rate*. This consisted of a medical examination of the patient and medication to manage the disease. A few medications that the general practitioner could not afford to dispense, he would then write out a prescription, for the patient to purchase from the pharmacist. This meant that not many prescriptions were written for my products, and for me to overcome this debacle, it meant heavy sampling, as this would give the doctor a chance to try out my products. This was a long term goal, but it paid off.

The medical-aid schemes were recently introduced and the private/general practitioner could afford to prescribe or dispense expensive medicines for their patients. The private/general practitioner did not take long to accept me and I soon started to be a recognizable figure within the pharmaceutical industry.

Several happenings were foreign to me, as I was amongst the few black ladies on the road within the pharmaceutical industry.

I could only see the doctor per appointment, which meant that the one trip was made specifically to secure an appointment, and the other trip was for the actual business.

There were call-cards that were to be filled in about the doctor's initial response after detailing him on the products. These call-cards were then filed alphabetically by the names of the doctors in a folder, which was to be kept in the boot of the car. Then everytime (i.e.) at six weekly intervals, a follow up would be made, and the doctor's response would be recorded in the call-cards. This was also a long term objective, which was aimed at winning the doctor's support for your company's products.

This was similar to report writing that was done in the nursing profession, whereby monitoring the patient's progress twice or thrice a day was vital. I found this process to be very helpful as it assisted me to set specific objectives for each encounter with the doctor and simultaneously monitor the progress made thus far.

Once in four to six weeks the manager would accompany the representative to work in the field for the day.

The representatives named this a *microscopic* day because on this day the representative was being placed under a microscope and every action was being scrutinized by the manager.

A few days following this exercise, the manager would then write an appraisal on the representative's performance, this process was repeated quarterly. These appraisals would later be reviewed and be used as recommendation for promotion. This also reminded me of my nursing days, that every month-end, the charge-nurse had to write a report on each and every nurse's performance, and this report would also be used later on as a recommendation and this was nerve wrecking.

I had been in the field for several months, I had studied my area, and knew it very well, by that I mean I knew my clients very well, whenever we were below budget, my manager would not hesitate to inform me, and I knew exactly whom to obtain the business from.

I was very fortunate in that I had a very supportive manager, because whenever he worked with me, he would always throw in positive comments, which were very encouraging. He would never criticize me in the presence of my clients, unlike the other managers, whenever they had a chance, they would really make a show-down or embarrass the representative. Somehow I remember my first national sales conference, as an incentive, the company had taken us to a place in the Eastern Transvaal called Bophelo Lodge for ten days, then I was not aware that none of the ladies (colleagues) were willing to share a room with me, but all I knew was that I occupied a room all by myself, I enjoyed this freedom as I did whatever I chose to do at my own moment and time, (e.g.) watching television channels of my choice, I could go swimming in the pool under the moonlight, I was in-charge of my little hotel room.

On our return from conference I once more put everything into my work, for me this was the best encouragement, because there was no way that I could afford such entertainment.

I actually enjoyed working outside than working in the office, like days when we had what was known as PCM or MCM (i.e. pre and post-cycle or mid-cycle meetings). On these days sales figures were being reviewed and if the sales figures were found to be below budget, this then warranted a total review of the marketing strategies and expense budgets. In this company I had established an excellent relationship with the telesales lady, whenever I had urgent orders I would simply phone through and the orders would be delivered promptly.

I really appreciated her services of which I would bring her gifts whenever we went on an overseas conference.

Through the knowledge gained from the marketing course, I had learnt techniques as to how to keep customers happy. Some of the things I did, was to invite my clients and their spouses out for dinner. Sometimes I would provide them with tickets for them to watch a soccer match, or I would provide them with tickets to attend shows at the Market Theatre, or if there were overseas artists who would be performing in South Africa, which was a very rare treat for South Africans during those days, to their delight, tickets would be made available to them.

It was during my third year of employment with this company that I won the prize of being runner-up representative of the year, with this I was offered air tickets for two, to Mauritius and accommodation for one week at the Aero beach hotel, all at the company's expense. This was wonderful, I had never dreamt of such luxuries, not in my wildest dreams. As black representatives from different companies, we used to work out our six weekly planners in such a manner that the sixth week, three or four of us would work in Swaziland at the same time. The aim being for us to team-up and attack the area simultaneously, the rewards achieved from this strategy proved to be of great benefit for us and our companies. I loved gambling, knowing very well, that I seldom won, I would go mad on those armbands (gambling machines), even when I did win, it would be small amounts of money. In fact whenever I was due for my country trip, I looked forward to those evenings in the casino with other representatives, this was also viewed as a treat as there were no casinos in South Africa then, except in the so-called Bophutatswana (suncity), a Bantu-stand designated for Setswana speaking people. A little explanation on the bantu-stand, following the relocation of the masses according to the different ethnic groups, the government then sought to affiliate these ethnic groups of people to the Bantu-stands and there were several of them scattered around the country. These were dry patches of land, situated far from the city, and had very little opportunities for employment.

Our little family had grown and the girls had developed into young adults and the boys, one was in his adolescent stage and our youngest son was still at primary school. They were all achievers in their own way. We had also grown financially and we could afford a descent car and a three bedroom house in the so-called middle class residential areas.

During the early 1970's the government had sought to develop a black middle class, who would be seen as urban blacks who fitted in the higher income bracket, who could afford certain luxuries (e.g.) descent furniture, radio, television and who owned a car, had a good paying job, lived in a secluded area and would aspire to emulate the western way of living.

Designated areas that were earmarked for these developments were Diepkloof-extension and Selection Park in Pimville.

When these houses were built by independent contractors, we had desired to own one, but financially we were far from being ready.

Years later with both of us occupying slightly higher positions, my husband being an auditor with an independent company and myself a market research officer with my current company. With our combined income we could at last afford to take a loan and pay a monthly mortgage bond and still had some disposable income left.

We all enjoyed our new home in a new area, new neighbours, new environment and a much larger property and the cherry on top was that on completion of payments on the mortgage bond which lasted for twenty years, we would then obtain total ownership of the property. This was a rare achievement, remember some years back, the masses were stripped off, of their properties under the group areas act, which stipulated that non-European persons were prohibited from ownership of property in the proclaimed urban areas.

The new areas were what was formerly known as the white areas, they were very attractive, the sizes of these properties were large, and the structures were beautiful. Those who could afford entered into contracts with the financial institutions. The exodus from the townships into the new areas was notable.

This affected the schools in the townships, because the parents saw it befitting that their children attend the local schools within their residential areas. This was then accompanied by one more exodus of black children into the former white schools, now known as *Model-C* schools.

These were exciting times as the masses continued to occupy the land that was formerly proclaimed, prohibited areas for non-Europeans, the masses watched on, as the previous land owners moved out of the areas in droves.

A typical way for the black masses to show appreciation for any achievement, was through celebration. As soon as a black family moved into one of these areas, they would celebrate with friends, it would be called a private party celebrating with a few friends, but with the amount of noise endured by the neighbours, the status quo would be questionable. Invariably the irritable neighbours would notify the police who would not hesitate to interrupt the celebration unceremoniously.

The following year I again won the prize of being runner-up representative of the year with the same package, I had aimed at winning the prize of being 'the representative of the year'. When this was being repeated for the third time I was not at all pleased, because I had made extra preparations to ensure that I did make it this time. I immediately sensed that there was something sinister, as I did check my sales figures on a weekly basis. The last time I checked on my sales figures was in October month and I was leading and the representative who was next in line was far behind me, I was actually ahead of him by several thousands of Rands.

I had gone on holiday in December month for two weeks and in January the following year during the national sales conference, which was held in Singapore, it was then that I learnt that some other representative had won the prize of being representative of the year. I was frustrated, I could not ask anyone as my manager had left the company at the end of December month. In that case I had no one to consult as my new manager was not au fait with whatever transpired.

I then confronted the national sales manager who tried hard to convince me. My next step was the marketing director, I would not say I knew him very well, but somehow I had some faith in him. I could recall those dark days, whenever we had visitors from America (i.e. the mother-body), I would be prepared before hand, I would be called in and be asked whether I was happy with the current setup and my work, and if not I would be asked specifically by the marketing director to say that I was indeed happy, and in return I would be rewarded for playing along, not that I was unhappy, but there would be these annoying incidences that would upset me.

I knew that this was a dangerous game that I was playing, I had been politicized sufficiently, I knew my rights I had taught myself to resist discrimination and oppression. Whenever I was faced with dealing with such difficult situations, I would ask myself, how ready was I to make this sacrifice, invariably I fell short.

I knew that I was failing my commitment and I was allowing all these attractions to interfere with my judgment, the question was, *"were the stakes exceeding the gains?"*

The marketing director seemed rather unsure as to how to handle the situation, he preferred to call me to his office, two days later. This gave me an opportunity to review the possibilities that were used to convince me otherwise. The sales figures were shown to me, and they tallied with mines up until October month, the November sales figures proved to be incorrect or rather skew. The December month's sales figures were reflecting a worse scenario, when I insisted on viewing the representative of the year's sales figures, the very same picture was reflected. According to the sales figures this particular representative's sales figures seemed to gain momentum during November-December months, which I instantly questioned.

According to my experience, I knew for a fact that ninety percent (90%) of the private practitioners did not buy bulk or large stocks as they were not willing to stock up their shelves as this was money tied down to shelve stocks and another reason they were also going on holiday and so were the patients and sometimes depending on the area they were also victims of burglaries. It was unquestionable that the books had been tampered with for obvious reasons (no black person shall supersede a white person), these were rules laid down on the statutory books of the country. I immediately recalled that phrase or a subsection of the job reservation act enhancing white supremacy.

The prize for the winner was two air tickets to Philadelphia in the U.S.A, at head office (mother-body) for one week and another week was reserved to visit all the other branches in America and sight seeing of all important places in U.S.A (United States of America). I was definitely anticipating for this trip as I watched my sales figures rocketing sky high and having decided to take my leave in December month, knowing very well that whoever was trailing behind me, had no chance of catching up.

Therefore this was a terrible blow, I had an option to hire a private investigator, but company policy deterred this move, sales figures were treated as highly confidential material and not to be divulged to the public. This man-made catastrophe I shared with my husband who encouraged me to work harder and prove them wrong, of which I was no longer prepared.

This made me very resentful and rebellious, my day to day performance was also affected, it almost destroyed my character.

In the meantime our children had grown, our eldest daughter was about to complete her degree, our second daughter was in her final year matriculation, our eldest son was in high school and our youngest son was in standard five. We had in the meantime moved house, from one area to another, looking at better surroundings and the distances we travelled daily to and from work, and also looking at better schools for the boys especially our youngest son, whose school performance had become unsatisfactory.

Considering my work situation that had become unbearable, I once more placed my c.v. in the market place, by end of that year, I had had a few offers from several pharmaceutical companies, including a direct recruitment from my former managers and this time around I decided to consider joining a German company.

During this time there were talks and news in the media locally and internationally of disinvestment, multinational companies were pressurized to pull-out of South Africa, as a means to try and force the South African government to abandon the apartheid laws that governed the country. Those were turbulent times, for most South Africans, the future looked bleak. My company being an American company was heavily impacted, so by end of the same year the company decided to merge with a British company, thus saving the situation of joblessness and unemployment. During that time several companies were forced to retrieve their businesses from the country. Some companies were bought by large South African companies under different names, and others offered their employees, what was known as a golden hand-shake (packages or benefits for services rendered over a certain period).

There were also other opportunities that were made available to the masses. The large business companies that were dealing in the property markets, had successfully applied to create a new type of property ownership in the form of holiday resorts which were being leased under the ninety-nine year lease contract. These properties took the form of hotels, that were divided into units, depending on the size of the hotel, then further divided into weeks for the whole year. A unit consisted of a lounge, kitchenette, a bathroom and two bedrooms, this unit would then be allocated for fifty-two weeks, (i.e.) this unit would be occupied by different owners every week for the whole year.

We were invited to a presentation on timeshares and having had some knowledge on the topic we took interest and indicated that we would soon be ready. A few years later we bought a timeshare unit in Durban overlooking the beach, this was one of our greatest investments, as our holiday was secure year after year.

We had established a second home for our family tov share and enjoy each other's company in a more relaxed atmosphere every year.

We would book in on a Saturday at ten o'clock in the morning, have a shower, have something to eat and later in the afternoon we would join other timeshare owners on the balcony for a welcome party organized by the owners of the hotel. The rest of the week would be spent on the beach, travelling around and sometimes we would travel to the Wildcoast sun in Transkei to enjoy a game of gambling. Remember that these gambling casinos were only permitted to operate in the Bantu-stands or homelands and this part of the country was designated for xhosa speaking people.

We sometimes swapped the unit for a different venue, depending on whether the particular hotel had a contract with the timeshare conglomerate, this too was a remarkable experience, we were able to visit many places during this timeshare swapping as it was called. During one of these swapping we visited Zimbabwe. We occupied a unit at the Troubeck motel on the border of Zimbabwe and Botswana.

In the evening we would enjoy watching the wild animals with the aid of a pair of binoculars, some grazing, some engaged in a fight and others enjoying a meal, a freshly killed prey. We would occasionally space-bank our week, thus accumulating our holiday time for the following year. The yearly fee (levy) was reasonable, the cost of travelling was not much because according to company policy I was allowed a full tank of fuel on my last day of work (i.e.) prior resuming holiday.

These were good times, family time was well spent and hope that our children would later in their lives have fond memories.

CHAPTER IV

Realizing my strengths

I never looked back, I started with my new company in January the following year. In this new company some faces were familiar, some were from my previous company, others I knew from being in the field or the market place, the former did not please me much, though I know it should be the other way around, in reality one should be pleased to re-unite with former colleagues. In the German company things were done differently, the perks (benefits overall) as they were named by the representatives were good, but had no provision for the education of the employees' children. It was company policy, that everybody who was a representative was allocated a jetta/csx only, except those who were ranked as principal representatives who were allocated the jetta/cli, and only the managers were allocated B.M.W's. I was offered the position of a hospital representative considering my experience, but the set-up remained the same. The principles were the same, I was employed to promote my products only in the black hospitals, which were scattered all over the Johannesburg region. Hospitals that were allocated to me, were; Galeshweng hospital, south of Pretoria, Meloding and Ladumahospitals which were also based in Pretoria, Selekeng hospital in Vergenoeg, Tshepanong hospital in Klerksdorp and Nampie hospital in East Rand. I also had two military hospitals as these were in my area. These hospitals were far apart. I travelled +/-250 kilometers a day, initially this was hard work as most of these hospitals had either never been serviced or inadequately serviced. The one aspect that fascinated me most with this position, was the fact that I would travel +/-110 kilometers to Klerksdorp and work in Tshepanong hospital and would drive back, and my white colleague would also drive another +/-110 kilometers to work in the white hospital in Klerksdorp and would drive back, exactly the very same procedure would be repeated in Selekeng/Vergenoeg hospital, Galeshweng/H.J.K. Marikie hospital etc. Invariably the same doctors rendered dual services to the hospitals, this meant that the same doctors who took care of the white patients in the white hospitals also took care of the black patients in the black hospitals. Considering the fact that these trips were also based on six weekly cycles. On the other hand this had some advantage to the company, the doctor would hear more frequently about the same products, and would then mean that once the doctor gained confidence in the product, the tendency to prescribe it as often as possible was very likely. I often asked myself, could management not devise a strategy that would reduce this duplication, this redundancy for a much simpler and much user friendly system that would be beneficial to the company, as this was most extravagant in terms of time, fuel consumption, human and material resources, it was definitely not one of the most effective methods of managing a company.

Amongst my colleagues who were kind enough to show me around, was an Irish lady, who with the advent of time became my friend. We related very well to each other, we basically understood each other. Our boss realized that and he would allocate us to share some of the large hospitals especially during a tea-room session. These tea-room sessions would sometimes be very large and this made it difficult to attend to each and every medical practitioner. However when it was two (2) of us we each would address a group at a time and be able to render a proper detail on our products. We had become inseparable. Whenever we went on sales conferences our boss made sure that we were allocated in one room as these were sharing rooms. My children once challenged me about this friend of mine that I always talked about. This was a real challenge, so I decided to invite her to our home and introduced her to my family, who did welcome her with open arms. She was a single woman, who had no children and the rest of her family lived in Ireland. She lived in a cottage in one of the suburban areas which was very near our work place. She was very neat and particular, especially concerning her dress code, her facial make-up, her perfume and her car, which was always well kept.

Somehow she reminded me of my mother's former employer.

She always told me about her frail mother, who was living alone in their family house, whilst her brothers who were married stayed somewhere in Dublin, this reminded me of my own mother, who at one stage was also staying alone.

She regularly telephoned her family to reassure them and to find out about her mother's condition.

When I got promoted, to the position of market research executive, she was overjoyed and she would visit me whenever she was at the office for some business. On one of her visits she told me that her mother was ill and that she needed to return to Ireland. She immediately started to prepare herself, by selling some of her belongings and her apartment.

The sad day of her departure had arrived and I had to see her off, this was another sad day for me, we had to part ways, six thousand (6,000) miles apart. This meant that seeing each other would be very costly and a rare opportunity.

We had developed this sisterly-hood relationship, whereby we shared most of the problems we encountered as individuals.

All hospital representatives were provided with pagers, at first I enjoyed this status quo, but it soon dawned on me that these fancy gadgets were a real menace, as the manager would use them to summon us into office at any odd time of the day.

These hospitals were mainly run by white doctors except in Galeshweng hospital, where the staff were comprised mainly of black doctors and nurses, the idea of working in black or white hospitals only, was far from reality.

I had to work out a strategy to prove my commitment to the doctors, and at the same time gain their confidence. I started off by creating specific clinic days which were utilized for teaching the patients about their condition (asthma) as a disease entity, the prognosis and the treatment, and their roles as patients in assisting the doctor in the management of the condition and finally to assist them as patients to lead a normal life as much as possible. A bit about the methods that were used to promote our products as hospital representatives. Our clients were highly professional people, so the methods used were also highly sophisticated. An appointment would be made to see the head of the department or the professor to detail him on your products, invariably they would have read about the products in the medical journals, which meant a brief detail highlighting only salient points. Another form would be a tea-room session, whereby products and promotional material would be displayed and cakes would be provided for the doctors.

A session could either be conducted on a one on one basis or a group presentation, whereby the doctors would sit and enjoy their tea and cakes whilst the representative would show a video on a particular product or give an oral presentation and would make time for questions.

On this particular day I was working with my manager and the tea-room session involved a group of physiotherapists, the presentation went well and I was about to sum-up, when my manager decided to interrupt me without any warning and he basically re-invented the wheel. This upset me very much, I excused myself and went to the toilet, I thought to myself now that he had decided to take over, he might as well do the wrap up. When I finally got out, I found him waiting with everything in his hands and some under his armpits. The first thing he uttered was "I'm sorry I only realized later what I had done". I was astonished by his behavior, the question was what was he trying to demonstrate to these physiotherapists, who happened to be white. The question was how on earth did I manage to be so successful, because during my short span with the company, I had managed to place two (2) products on the then T.P.A. (Transvaal Provincial Administration) open code.

A brief explanation, T.P.A. regulations were such that a product could either be placed on restricted code or open code, the latter meant that the product was freely available to the nurses and the doctors only on prescription. Whilst with the former, the doctors had to write out a motivation for the drugs that they needed and this was time consuming. Having had two products on open code was a great achievement for me and for my company.

My very first two years with this company was a success, budgets were exceeded by a good margin. All the representatives received an incentive payout accompanied by a trip to Singapore, where we occupied one of the most expensive hotels. This hotel was situated in the middle of the city surrounded by an abundance of shopping malls. The one dealer approached our managing director and made an offer of 25% discount on all goods purchased from his store. By the time we left this store, it was emptied of music systems, cellular phones, cameras, video machines etc. Everyone had large wrapped parcels and these were transported separately via shipment.

I used this opportunity to the fullest as this was my second time around, I knew exactly what I wanted (e.g.) a fax machine, a music system with a c.d. player, a video camera and a few electronic items for the children. The boys made good use of the video camera to obtain pocket money for school trips and other school activities.

The following year we were set to have our conference in Barley, but unfortunately we did not make budget and the company settled for an African state. It was standard with this company, that we enjoyed the national sales conferences outside South Africa, these were real good times.

The company had the privilege of being headed by a very proactive c.e.o. who was forever in search of new products to be brought over to the South African market, hence the launch of new products almost every year, which was accompanied by excessive growth even when the rest of the pharmaceutical market was reflecting a negative growth.

The rest of my family had in the meantime moved up to the Transvaal to join my elder sister and brother. A few years later my younger sister and brother got married and were also staying in the township. My mother was no longer working, and as a family we tried to supplement her monthly pension funds, but with very little success. According to the apartheid regulations, blacks were only to reside in the townships, whilst employed, but as soon as they retired (no longer of service to their masters), they had to be sent to the homelands. A clarification of these homelands, when an application was made for an I.D. (identification document), automatically the ethnic grouping would be affiliated to a homeland.

Our family belonged to the Northern Sotho/Pedi ethnic group and we were automatically linked to the former Lebowa, of which Pietersburg was part of. As much as we hated this system, we saw it as an advantage at the time. Our mother had grown old, she could no longer cope with city life. Maintaining her and our own homes had become very costly, we then decided to build her a reasonably sized house in her village in Pietersburg. She was overwhelmed and pleased to re-unite with some of her relatives and old friends who were still alive.

Whenever we visited her, she would organize corn mealies from her garden, after peeling off the layers, these would then be roasted on an open fire. This was a real treat especially for people who spent most of their time in the city, who were now enjoying freshly roasted corn mealies sitting in front of an open fire, how wonderful!.

My younger sister's husband had political tendencies and he subsequently became an activist and during the Soweto uprising, he was amongst those who were arrested and was subsequently imprisoned for several years. This then left my younger sister with serious problems, she had five children to take care of, and this proved to be a mammoth task for a single parent. As a family we once more decided that three (3) of the children should join our mother in Pietersburg and that they would be of great help and company to her. My mother was still physically very strong, however we thought that she might appreciate the company of her grand-children. Their ages ranged between six and thirteen years, they were all of school going age and were very responsible. We took turns in visiting them, this was just to ensure that things were running smoothly.

This was one of the best investments we made as a family. The three children grew up with very little influence from the city, they attended school very well and finally completed their schooling. One of the children was very goal oriented, she pursued her studies further and had graduated as an auditor.

Several years later my mother became ill and she passed on at the age of eighty-two (82) years. What a blessing!.

CHAPTER V

New era

Once more the country was going through turbulent times, South Africans were being scattered all over the world again, a real exodus of a wide variety of professionals, new investments into the country were very declining by the day, the situation was most unpredictable. A powerful political organization was being unbanned and there was word going around that this was the ruling party in waiting. The fact of the matter was that white South Africans had ruled the country for 40+ years and were now anticipating problems with the possibility of a black government ruling the country. All sorts of negative comments were made, like South Africa will become a banana republic just like the rest of the African states and that there would be blood-shed, it was not going to be an easy take over. Communication between members of the current government and those of the political organization were such that smooth negotiations seemed impossible. The then current prime minister of the country was then replaced and suddenly the people of the country could see the light at the end of the tunnel. A positive move in the right direction was immediately made. The announcement on television of the imminent release of several high profile political leaders, startled the country.

Volatility and uncertainty prevailed in the country for some time. On the actual day of the release, the masses went into a celebration mood, the streets in the townships were filled with people who were running, dancing and singing, this was a typical African way that the masses expressed their joy or appreciation.

This was a very fragile phase in our country, as prominent activists who were fighting the apartheid regime were assassinated, one after the other.

The exodus of mainly the white community of South Africa continued and those who remained in the country, were probably or most likely in support of a black government and had over the years made many sacrifices, and had paid dearly for their beliefs. The others had probably not anticipated for any real change and had adopted the wait and see attitude.

The white community of South Africa consisted mainly of the descendants from the Dutch settlers of 1652, the 1820 British settlers, the French huguenots, and from several other European countries (e.g.) the Netherlands, Spain, China e.t.c. They had lived in South Africa for centuries and probably some of them no longer had ties with their families in Europe.

The whole country watched in awe as we were all seated in front of the television screens as the negotiations were unfolding, between the then current government and the government in waiting. We the masses are not politicians, but from a layman's point of view, things appeared as if barriers that were built over the years could not be easily broken.

Remember that the one group, comprised of the *citizens* of the country, whilst the other group comprised of *terrorists*, and now they were sitting at opposite sides of the same negotiating table, facing each other, man to man, eyeball to eyeball as they were trying very hard to broker a deal, that would be beneficial to all South Africans.

As the uncertainty prevailed, so did the exodus into the European countries and these were accompanied by the financial losses, as stated earlier on the white community had the economical power and had secured the perpetual sustenance of this status quo over the years.

Following deliberations and discussions between the political organization and the current government, a voting date was set and this was announced on television and the media.

On the 27th April 1994 all South Africans went to the polls to vote, this was a very memorable and a very significant day in the lives of most South Africans. Black and white South Africans stood together at the voting polls, for the very first time in the history of our country. We all stood side by side next to each other, each one secretly knowing which party would gain the indelible mark the 'x', to indicate the party of choice. An expression of joy by one pensioner read thus "she had been pregnant for a long, long time and had finally given birth", a simple phrase to express the birth of the new South Africa.

People of my colour had never before had the right to cast a vote and were seeing ballot papers for the very first time, and needed assistance in terms of the paper work that was required, and this was well done by the queue marshals. (the young comrades)

The outcome was that this political organization had won by a two thirds majority, this was a popular political organization, well known by the masses. The parties involved immediately resumed with further negotiations in terms of the handing over of power. There were several disruptions and distractions during this delicate phase, however the negotiating process had to be continued to the end.

The dawn of this day brought along with it many hopes, many dreams and many aspirations for many South Africans, especially the down trodden and I was no exception.

I was already in my late forties, and was looking forward for some form of approval by way of a promotion, I had not forgotten the apartheid regime, which I did not expect to disappear overnight and that my chances of becoming a manager were very slim. I started off by applying in the very company that I was working for, and after a few months of waiting, I decided to place my c.v. in the market place and I started attending interviews as usual. One interview which was unforgettable, the marketing manager seemed impressed with me during our telephonic conversation and an appointment was made for me to meet with him. I arrived at the company half an hour earlier, I had made sure that I looked very presentable, all in all I wanted to impress him. As the secretary ushered me in, I could see that he seemed disappointed, but because I was already there, he had to salvage the situation by asking the secretary to make copies of my c.v. and my certificates and he dismissed me, giving me the impression that he still had several more applicants to interview. This to me was definitely a negative step, I then persevered in the line of product manager, though I knew of only one black lady who was a product manager for an American company, but when the particular company decided to retrench the staff, she happened to be one of the first to be relieved of her duties. Some companies insisted on experience as a product manager and availability to travel overseas on a regular basis.

In the pharmaceutical and multinational companies it was a norm for these companies to travel overseas for conferences at the head-quarters once or twice a year, whereby each country is represented, marketing structures are laid out, budgets are set, feedback on current performances are also stated in detail. During these conferences, the managing director of the company would present the performance of his total company for his country, the national sales manager and the product managers, the former would present sales figures and market shares and performance of the total company, and the latter would then present a breakdown on the performances of the individual products. A brief explanation (i.e.) out of a large cake, slices are cut and allocated to each country according to the country's previous year's actual sales. These are worked out in percentages (e.g.) 100% would be total company budget for the whole world, (i.e.) where the company had business structures in place, (e.g.) fifteen countries would contribute 6,67% each and these would be converted into the relevant currency.

Things were changing very fast within the company, I was told that before the current managing director (c.e.o.) took over, the company was about to close down. The managing director came from the far east countries, to me he seemed a firm person who took no nonsense from anyone and was also very target orientated. Once or twice I had the opportunity to talk to him, he would ask me questions, like "how's business? how's a particular product doing in the market place?", questions like these told me that he was also a driver type of a leader.

In this company management positions were held mainly by white males, the sales force seemed evenly distributed.

I recalled when I was still working for my previous company, I used to meet the representative from this German company, he was a hard worker but very unhappy, he always complained about his immediate boss, and that he was racist in his approach. I knew for a fact, that he was very thinly spread as I would meet him on my every second or third cycle, and he was the only black representative in his company and was working in all the black states, black hospitals and all the townships, he had a massive area to cover.

When I joined the company there were lots of changes, I took over the position formerly held by the only black representative as he was then promoted to management.

I had gained a lot of experience and confidence from my previous American company. I had also learnt to speak my mind, so I carefully laid out some of my employment conditions (e.g.) no country trips, no independent/black states and only hospitals that allowed me to drive in and out on a daily basis. As mentioned that my predecessor was promoted to management and he was made manager of two black representatives. Once more the apartheid strategy came to the fore, whilst the other three managers had eight to ten (8-10) representatives reporting to them. I once more questioned this kind of management, could the workload not be evenly distributed, or was he not good enough to be made in charge of white representatives, then why the camouflage?

Some of the changes involved the transfer of the national sales manager to the far east countries, the one manager was sent to the far north and the other manager was sent to the far east/west countries, thus the creation of positions for those who needed to climb up to the higher ranks within the company. Almost a year later I received a reply from the marketing director, who was keen to know what progress I had made in regards my studies and whether I was computer literate.

I remember when computers were launched in the country by a company named Ur.Machine. I was still a nursing sister and I judged the P.C's to be some complicated equipment out there, designed for the highly skilled people in the financial institutions and the economics world.

I was finally offered the job of being a market research executive and I was to commence duties, five months later the following year. I was overjoyed with this kind of response, at least this would allow me to continue with my services in the same company.

It later came to my attention that I was not the only person within the company who was anxiously awaiting a reply concerning promotion, this was my new boss in waiting.

My new boss in waiting when he was still a group product manager, always asked for my assistance with the interpretation of the I.S.C. data as he was not familiar with the codes. We (myself and my boss) would work for hours, two to three (2-3) days a week in his office, interpreting the market shares and filling in volumes and volumes of work sheets pertaining to marketing strategies.

I also learnt that the c.e.o.was given this mammoth task from head office, overseas, and the c.e.o saw it fit to delegate the task to my boss as the prospective marketing manager and he in turn saw it fit to involve me. I was fully committed to this mammoth task to the very end. Little did I realize that sooner or later, my new boss would be baying for my blood. I do not have any regrets or hard feelings over this, but I thought if only I could have been treated with some respect.

I immediately underwent training on the use of P.C's which was done within the company by a very friendly lady. This reminds me of one day as she was passing my office and she could hear me clicking away on the keyboard as I was busy typing, she remarked that "I never thought that you'll be able to type", this was a real compliment. I also had to undergo training on the use of I.S.C. (international surveillance company) data. This is an independent organization, which compiles data for the whole pharmaceutical industry in South Africa and is internationally linked. I.S.C. provides data related to the pharmaceutical market by company and by product.

Subscriptions were being paid by the individual companies in order to secure their monthly copies of data, which was printed monthly, quarterly, bi-annually and annually and even every five yearly.

In June the same year, I had to produce my first copy on the price competitor analysis, which was made available to the sales representatives quarterly. I could recall how valuable I had found this piece of documentin the market place, and this motivated me to ensure that, it was accurate and consisted of relevant information.

On acceptance of the position, I was given a contract for the position, this consisted of a two page document with details relating to my job description. This was given to me by the human resource manager, I still do not know whether this was an interview to assess my capability for the position or was it an interrogation. Things that were said to me on that particular day, were most appalling, some of the things, were that I had studied for personal gain and that the company did not employ representatives to turn them into managers.

This infuriated me, because I knew for a fact that 70% of the company's managers started off as sales representatives.

I decided to handle this matter very cautiously. According to company policy any private studies done, entitled one to reimbursement. I knew this would definitely, upset him, so I proceeded to submit my claim forms for the three year course.

In order for the claim to be processed, receipts were required, of which I could not produce, because the studies were done privately over a period of four years. This turned out to be a nightmare for me, however the college came to my rescue.

I finally submitted my receipts and received my payout, I did not consider this a victory, but I was looking for a way to report him to the marketing director, however I anticipated for our paths to cross once more and sooner, of which I thought was very unlikely.

Whenever the human source manager visited our department (marketing department) he would visit my boss and one of the product managers. They would chat and laugh loudly ignoring the fact that other employees on the same floor were busy working. The topic was always about his favourite rugby team. I had very little knowledge about rugby, but whenever his favourite team had won, I would see him walk down the stairs tomy boss's office to share his joy over his team's achievement. In the townships rugby was seen as a sport played mainly by strong, well-built white-men, and was only played in the suburban areas, where there were large, well maintained sports fields. Whilst soccer was the most popular sport amongst the masses, this sport would be played in the dusty streets of the township and whenever certain major teams were playing, these major events would be hosted in poorly maintained and dilapidated soccer stadiums.

I was unhappy with my new office, one of the personal assistants had swapped her office for mine, under the pretext that she needed a bigger office to store her files. I returned to the marketing director, I don't know whether he was avoiding conflict, but he granted me permission to relocate myself somewhere upstairs, of which I did and I eventually settled down. This gave me an opportunity to concentrate on my work, I explored the various programs and discovered several methods of tackling my job. I really got stuck into my work, I produced graphs on the monthly sales figures which were interpreted in rands and units.

The group product manager was a pleasant person to work for, he had drawn out guidelines which I had to adhere to, in regards which sales figures, were to be made available to the managers. These sales figures consisted of two sets (i.e.) one set consisted of in-house data and the other set consisted of data as mentioned from I.S.C.

All this data had to be graphically interpreted, copies to be distributed to the various product managers. The group product manager, I must say was an experienced person for the position. Once a week on Mondays we held meetings whereby we were updated about each member's activities for the week, (e.g.) training of newly employed representatives, congresses, feedbacks on any new developments pertaining to the marketing team. I was kept well informed on most of company's activities, I really appreciated this set-up, this also enhanced my sense of belonging.

In one of these meetings, my boss decided to convene a meeting between marketing and sales department, whereby the sales department were asked what they would like to see reflected on the graphs so that they would be more specific and meaningful to them. I was amazed at the suggestions that emanated from this meeting. In addition to what was already available, they required graphs that reflected the current sales figures versus those of the previous year, in order to detect the variance which would reflect, either a positive or negative growth, however these sales figures were already provided monthly via the in-house data. This was obviously a lot of work and duplication of services and it left me with no room for any ad hoc research, nor viability studies nor any validation studies, I had to outsource these whenever necessary.

My day started at 08h00 and finished at 17h00 doing my best to adhere to the deadlines, I literally stared at my computer for nine hours, less my lunch and tea breaks (1h30minutes). This continued for some time, once more I viewed this exercise as another way of trying to frustrate me and I knew for a fact that they, the sales managers would not find the time to analyze all the graphs, and that they would probably look at a few or only those of interest and the rest would be filed in file 13 (discard). This matter was raised in one of the marketing meetings to no avail. This to me was a real waste of time, material and human resources, again could management not utilize my services more effectively.

Conference in Swazi Land

Husband playing golf

Matema and her colleague in Mauritius

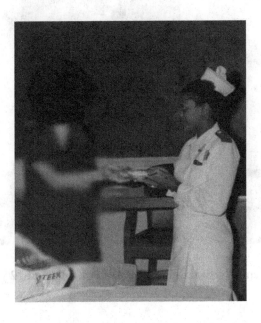

Matema receiving an award for best performance in
Nursing Administration

Matema, Ntswara-ngwako and son Lephato at 12 years
and 6 years respectively

Matete our eldest son at the age of 17 years

Mosholadi our eldest daughter at the age of 4 years

CHAPTER VI

Changing times

I was now very involved in a futile exercise, I was excluded from attending meetings, I was basically left in limbo, all I did was to print volumes and volumes of material on sales graphs, and whenever someone entered my office I already knew that he had come to highlight an error that I had made. From my nursing experience I was well trained to acknowledge criticism positively and to respond with instant rectifications, I did manage to overcome this. Each day passed by like any other day, the excitement of being in the office was gradually wearing off. Some of the changes that took place within the company, I heard from the tea ladies and the warehouse staff who were mainly black, or whenever I had a spare moment to trod downstairs to read the notices on the notice board. The secretaries kept to themselves most of the time, and I had enough on my plate to keep me busy.

The company started employing new representatives as a sign of expansion and growth. These were highly qualified university graduates who had no previous work experience, but were prepared to apply their text book knowledge. They were vibrant and well informed about the pharmaceutical markets. I watched as what I would label, *A tug of war* which ensued. The older group of managers had ample experience and wished to apply their autocratic ideas and methods of doing things, whilst the newly employed graduates resisted and perceived these ideas and methods as being out dated.

The older group of managers consisted of white males, who had no medical background, but due to the knowledge and experience they accumulated over the years, they were able to manage very well in their respective portfolios. They belonged to the category that was rarely challenged and that enjoyed the protection of the job reservation act, whereby certain jobs were only to be occupied by white people. Whilst the younger group of managers were knowledgeable, open minded and technically advanced.

They were also goal oriented, they saw themselves rising up the echelons within the pharmaceutical industry within a short space of time. Under these circumstances, things became stagnant, as we would spend days arguing as to which marketing strategy to adopt, with very little success and without reaching any definite conclusions.

The intervention by the company executives brought about the much awaited change. The older managers were then relocated to other duties within the company. What a relief!.

It so happened that one morning as I was taking my car to the garage, I was involved in an accident, it was God's will that I managed to be thrown out of the moving car, as it rolled down the street on its own into a big tree. This was a complete right-off and I was booked off-sick for six weeks.

I sustained serious injuries, my knees, elbows and the back of my skull were badly lacerated. However on x-ray there were no fractures detected.

I did recuperate and returned to work, where I was awakened by bad news that, the insurance brokers found that I was to be blamed for the accident, and this meant that I had to incur all costs. This annoyed me very much, my argument being that the car was faulty and I was on my way to the garage. I might have viewed things from a different perspective, because I was due for a new car and this issue was being used as an excuse to try and frustrate me. I was then offered a pool car which I drove for nine months, as management could not decide what car or rather under which rank to place me. The human resource manager, had in the meantime gone to Head-office, overseas to undergo training in human resource management, from my perspective this was a joke. Some of the human resource manager's duties were to ensure that all employees of the company belonged to a medical-aid scheme. What I could remember, was that for the three years that I had been with the company, we had changed from one medical-aid to another. Batho-kaofela medical-aid scheme was one of them and I used to complain bitterly about them.

They seldom reimbursed the members in time, prescriptions that were written for ethical drugs were being substituted with generic products, this was done without the member's permission. This particular medical-aid scheme had their members segmented according to the apartheid regime (i.e.) blacks/whites/indians/coloureds, each racial group had a special code as a means of identification and this meant different contributions and this was accompanied by different benefits.

Still on the subject of the human resource manager, which to this day, the question remains, whether this was indeed a worthwhile exercise for him or for his company in South Africa. In the meantime I had written a letter to my manager in regards aspects that concerned my job description (contract). The main issues were my portfolio per se, business cards, and my company car as all these were intertwined. There was also a lot of grapevine as mentioned, that I was the last person to gather any, (e.g.) the national sales manager was being transferred to the Far East, and lot more re-shuffling of the various management positions and that included the personal assistants as well. My turn to receive fresh or rather live grapevine arrived, part of the grapevine, was that I was debarred from attending the national sales conference which was to be held in Malaysia.

Initially I was very upset, but as I looked into the man's eyes I could see the hurt and that he himself had nothing to say, but his task was to carry out instructions from above (c.e.o.), to this day I have not been able to resolve this issue, the question was, was the c.e.o., negatively influenced, for him to make such a drastic decision. I knew for a fact that my predecessor used to attend all sales conferences. The question was, why this decision? was there some person within the company who wanted to frustrate me, and eventually push me out of the company?. Once more I was subjected to the subtle but oppressive behaviour of the people who were determined to keep the apartheid regime alive.

This decision affected me badly, I could sense the oppressive hands forcefully pushing me down and out, to a stage that I once more had my c.v. out in the market place.

I had done an intensive planning, my intentions were that by the time the rest of the company employees returned from conference, I would be tendering my resignation, a twenty four notice at that.

Having thought this through I realized that this was a very foolish plan and not at all feasible, because according to the contract, made between me and my employer, which clearly stipulated that on termination of services, either parties had to serve a month's notice to allow for complete and proper handing over of responsibilities.

I knew for a fact that the c.e.o. was also a shrewd businessman, but somehow he would show his appreciation for my good work, whilst I was still a sales representative. This reminds me of the Christmas parties sponsored by the company yearly, for the employees and their spouses to enjoy dinner at some exorbitant venues. The c.e.o. would ensure that my spouse and I were allocated to share a table with him and his wife and his executives and their partners.

I was also aware of the fact that this gesture was a thorn in the eyes of other employees within the company.

I somehow knew that I would be paying a heavy price for this accomplishment (i.e.) (sharing a table with the big boys within the company). It never occurred to me that the price would be this high, being told in no uncertain terms that "you will not be part of the team to the national sales conference this year", was the last thing I expected. On their return, two weeks later work resumed as usual, the group product manager, occupied the position of the national sales manager and his position was left vacant, so once more I had to report to the marketing director. I seldom spoke to this Englishman, he seemed a very cool, steady and a level-headed person. He involved me a lot in the research projects but not in the manager's meetings, once more I was left out of contact with the rest of the company. Six weeks later the marketing director, finally replied to my letter addressing the various issues which were of concern to me. I was then provided with another contract, which referred to my position as market research officer. The duties were exactly the same, except the portfolio itself.

I ended up having two sets of contracts with the same job description.

I was now very confused, because at no stage was I told that the latest contract superseded the former.

I was then provided with a new car, the same as that provided for the sales representatives, the question remained "was my promotion really meaningful or was it just another camouflage? or was it what some companies termed *window dressing?*". This phenomenon was rife during those years, when the South African companies were under great duress from their mother bodies, (head office overseas) which had protocols in place for companies that invested in Africa to grant blacks or (the indigenous people of the land) opportunities for employment and development in the workplace.

In trying to comply to these protocols the companies would employ black people, but would not hand over any responsibility nor any accountability. At the end of the day these black managers were being used to impress the overseas guests who were equally fooled by this artificial situation. I then analyzed both my contracts, specifically at the incumbent per se, which referred to it as market research executive (as stated in the first job description), which was later revised as market research officer (as stated in the second job description), the latter was specifically designed to fit in with the benefits and privileges that were granted. I was unhappy with this situation, but I had to let go, because, I had recently become very grumpy, like a dog suffering from a painful tooth.

Working in the office as a market research officer was a pleasant task, except for a few hiccups. The personal assistants to the managers behaved as if they owned the company. They knew far more than I did in terms of current events that happened within the company, that included the average grapevine, that was in circulation. The use of company facilities became a problem for me, these ladies claimed the company's properties as being their own, by using terms like my computer, my printer, my scanner, my copier e.t.c. The company had set printers to be shared by two-three users, this was a brilliant idea, as it was very economical and ensured maximum usage of equipment. However these ladies did not seem to be economically orientated, thus each personal assistant had a printer, a photocopy machine and a colourful printer fitted in their offices. I failed to understand, how their managers could allow such extravaganza, whilst there was a huge outcry to save on costs within the company.

This set-up placed me in a difficult situation, as my computer was linked to their printers. On appointment to this position, I was told that I could only have a printer the following year when the company would be due to order again in bulk.

I recall one personal assistant instructing me to print one copy of each graph and the rest I could make copies on the photocopy machine. I could clearly hear her say that, she did not appreciate me walking in and out of her office, the fewer the trips the better for her.

Another personal assistant suggested that I phoned her before printing, claiming that the material that I printed interfered with hers, again I could clearly hear her saying, that I was not welcomed to use her printer. Unfortunately for her, that morning I suppose I wasn't in the best of my moods, so I exploded, to my surprise she got very upset, this didn't deter me from informing her, that these were company assets and that I had the same right as much as anyone else.

I then reported this incident to the marketing director, and I subsequently wrote a detailed letter regarding all the other matters that were of concern to me. This matter was dealt with in detail, whereby the marketing director took the opportunity to discipline the personal assistant concerned. The ramifications were negative, the one lady was transferred to another department, to this day I really could not substantiate what else transpired, but all in all I appreciated the change of attitude towards me from the personal assistant that remained in the department.

The company was in the process of launching a new product, I was very involved in the beginning, but I later found out that the research and viability studies were done without my knowledge. Following a few rectifications, I managed to be updated with all the data, including the progress that had been made thus far. The company executives from head-office had visited us, and were interested to know what progress we had made in our preparation to launch the new product. I then had the privilege of presenting some of the research material that I had prepared on the new product to our overseas guests. I presumed that the presentation went very well, or the research material revealed information which was of great pertinence to a successful launch, because at lunch time, discussions revolved around the figures and the potential that the product reflected. I was now in full swing with this new product and I was also preparing myself to present the same material at the national sales conference, as told by the marketing director.

CHAPTER VII

Challenging times

The national sales conference was usually held at the beginning of each year to layout the foundations and to inform the managers and the sales representatives about the forecasts and the budgets for the current year and various other important announcements. I went on holiday knowing very well that I'll be going on the national sales conference. I therefore cut my holiday short, so that I could find sufficient time to prepare myself.

A little bit about my holiday of which I spent two weeks touring Egypt and Israel. I recalled that from my previous employments I had the privilege of visiting a lot of countries overseas, with a few exceptions and one of them was the holy-land. I suppose a company that would offer a trip to the holy-land, as an incentive is yet to be seen. Anyway I really enjoyed myself, as there was no pressure from anyone and the fact that the group consisted only of ladies. We spent three nights in Egypt, we visited places of significance, one that caught my attention, was the plantation, which was divided into blocks which were identifiable by the different colours of roses. During the processing time, the roses would be packed neatly according to their colours, in containers and ready for fermentation. Certain chemicals would then be added in order to produce perfumes of various fragrances. We bought a few perfumes that were ready for the market. We then proceeded to visit where the Egyptian mummies were kept, in their different sizes and shapes. The first and the last time I saw these mummies was when they were displayed as part of an advertisement on television. Standing there viewing the real mummies in their cages, was quite an experience, some were just too large, and they looked frightening, and I was not surprised that, that very evening I experienced some terrible nightmares.

There were also several factories, where disabled children were being trained to wove carpets, which were placed on the market at reasonable prices. We bought quite a few of these and they were sent back home by courier services.

We then proceeded with our journey and crossed over the Mediterranean sea by ferry, this was also a wonderful experience. We had booked into the Tel-Aviv hotel from where we spent the rest of the days touring interesting places, like visiting Jerusalem, River Jordan, the ruins of King Herod's castle, the dead sea, and many other exciting places.

Two weeks seemed a long time, but time passed on far too quickly and soon it was time to return home, but what a wonderful experience.

I resumed work nine days after new year's day, I had great plans aligned for the new year and how I was going to ensure that I maintained my position as part of the marketing team. However my plans were not even put into practice, when I was called by the group product manager, my new boss into his office. I was once more told that unfortunately the marketing director, had decided to exclude my name from the list of those who would be going on the national sales conference.

My little world once more crumbled around me, I was dump-stricken, I just sat there and stared into space. I could sense that my boss expected me to respond, and yet my mind was still struggling to deal with the agony. I sat there for a few minutes, as my manager, was trying very hard to convince me, or rather to brainwash me, claiming that there was no need for me to be at the national sales conference, as I only had one slide to present, of which was untrue. I was not in a mood to argue with him, firstly I judged that he had failed to handle such a sensitive matter in a dignified and non-biased manner.

I returned to my office, where I sat for a while trying to make sense out of the whole thing. I cannot recall for how long I sat in my office whilst my mind was pondering over several other issues. Hurt and anger was swelling up inside of me, I felt like lashing out at someone, but who? These were my bosses, they were responsible for sustaining my employment with the company and making sure that I remained employed.

My response to this, I was like a wounded dog trying to lick its wounds which were sustained during a fight with other dogs, except that in my case the fight was one sided, and I was on the receiving end.

I thought to myself afterall he was a white South African male and was not sensitive enough towards my feelings, being a black woman, who is not much different from his maid at his home. A maid is a black woman who exchanges her services for a wage, she does house duties for the madam of the house, she has no unemployment nor pension benefits, no maternity nor sick leave benefits, no overtime-pay the list is endless, to sum-up this category of labourers, they are some of the most exploited people in South Africa, and yet many a manager or directors of these large enterprises were invariably raised by these maids also known as nannies.

Employment seekers would have their names advertised under the column reserved for domestic employment. Details pertaining to the employment seeker would comprise of the name, type of job, be it nanny, housekeeper or a cook, the contact details and some references. The potential employer would then contact the employment seeker and arrange for an interview. They do not negotiate for wages, simply because they do not know how, but would accept whatever offer that is made to them. They fall under the category of unskilled labourers, ignoring the fact that these mothers, these wives are daughters of the soil of Africa.

They are being advertised on these newspapers, referring to them as maids, my-maid-Betty, note only first names are being used, no surnames or second names, no African names, they are being treated as some commodity available on the market and only for the white-man as he can afford to employ several of them.

In brief I'll try to paint a picture, depicting exploitation at its best, one employer can utilize the services of a nanny, a housekeeper, a cook, a garden-boy, (by the way this is my father), and a washing-girl (this is my mother) and perhaps a chauffeur, ignoring the fact that these people are all sons and daughters of this soil, who have been deliberately impoverished over the years.

I need to confess that I also know of a few well known political and social leaders of good standing in our communities who had the privilege of being sponsored throughout their educational careers by these employers, whilst their mothers were under the employment of these white families. "What a privilege!"

The situation had become most unbearable, I could no longer handle the psychological abuse, I was later asked to handover my slides on the new product to the group product manager, so that he could present them on my behalf. I was very apprehensive and was tempted to refuse, but on second thought I realized that it would not be a wise move, and that this kind of behaviour would be interpreted in many negative ways.

A few days before the group left for conference, I was called by my boss into his office to discuss my salary increment and he informed me, on how our mother-body in overseas expected management to be evaluated on their work performance. This amazed me, because the last time I had an appraisal done, was when I was still a sales representative and I always wondered to myself as to, how management worked out the incremental percentages on a yearly basis, or was this just a thumb suck. (figures pulled out of a hat) My manager once more asked me if I had anything to say, I could detect that there was a hidden agenda, once more no good intentions would derive from this. I once again found myself left in limbo. During this time I felt lonely, isolated from everybody else, I no longer knew the names of the sales representatives, as I rarely saw them.

Thinking back of a productive lifetime that was wasted, those blurry snap shots of phases in my life, within the company, are what I would later label as the difficult times that were embroiled by a dark cloud.

My husband and I had also decided not to join the rest of the company employees any longer for Christmas dinners, hoping and thinking, that this would send a strong message, as to how unhappy I was, as if they cared.

Whilst the group was on conference the monologue resumed once more, several interviews were attended, but I had to stop and do some introspection, my age, my responsibilities and other binding circumstances were becoming deterring factors.

One of the days whilst the group was still away on conference, I managed to drive to Janefurse (Limpopo) to place our youngest son at college. I just thought what a wonderful idea. This is a young man in his adolescent stage, he is easily influenced by his peers, he had started to do badly at school his yearly mark had deteriorated badly and we could not pinpoint the problem. We had changed him from one school to another, instead the problem became worse, and we found ourselves in a serious predicament. The only way at the time then, was to place him in a boarding school far away from home. The main objective of this exercise was to try and allow him to become self-sufficient, independent and partly to break away from the circle of friends.

Working as a market research officer, seemed a very comfortable job, as I was not working under any supervision of any kind, but what used to upset me most, was the fact that I was always left in limbo. I used to wander, was I still part of marketing, or was I someone working totally independent of the rest of the team, or was I being used as a beacon of hope for young aspiring sales representatives, by creating a false impression that the company provided equal opportunities for all.

I was gradually becoming a thorn in the eyes of those in authority, especially my boss, who never ceased to challenge the demeanor he saw in me, that was sometimes combined with a smack of arrogance that he depicted, every time we were in conflict.

One of the front ladies at the reception desk was in trouble with the authorities of the company. She was found eating her breakfast whilst operating the switchboard, this was not a good reflection of the company, a multinational company at that. She asked me to represent her at the disciplinary enquiry and that she was scared that she might lose her job, she also told me that she did not enjoy a good working relationship with her immediate boss.

I had become so rebellious that I ignored all possible dangers, red warning lights were flickering at me from all directions. I had decided to represent my fellow employee, and my argument was that it was her first offence, which would not be repeated, and could management consider her plea and at least give her a written warning. This disciplinary enquiry was attended by the presiding officer, the human resource manager and her boss who represented the company, myself and the receptionist.

The outcome was welcomed as she was given a written warning, at least her job was saved.

This was a reflection of my view of the company, I had lost respect for those in authority and sought to challenge them at any given opportunity and I was not taking cognizance of my own reputation being tarnished, nor the fact that my own job might be at risk.

The company had in the mean-time bought two large properties which were adjacent to the company. Building contractors were given the go ahead and resumed with the construction immediately. Within a period of less than a year everything was completed. The new buildings comprised of a double storied building, which was occupied by the self-medication (products that were sold over the counter) division, the medical information team and the medical research team. The former two (2) teams occupied the left wing on the upper and lower levels respectively, and the latter occupied the upper level on the right wing. On the ground floor was the office of the training manager and adjacent to it was the conference room/auditorium. This was where most of the meetings and other activities were held.

Another building, was a research division but was never fully utilized and the other building was a fully equipped gymnasium with a qualified gymnastics instructor, which the employees utilized at no cost of their own. Attached to the gymnasium on the left hand side was the canteen, which provided nutritious, appetizing meals, that were subsidized by the company. Attached to the gymnasium on the right hand side was a miniature lodge, this comprised of bedrooms which had bathrooms, and resting rooms. These were initially designed to accommodate the coastal managers who regularly came to Johannesburg to attend sales meetings.

These buildings were surrounded by beautiful gardens, that were well maintained through-out the year. In between these buildings were pathways that led from one building to the other and were decorated by beautiful flowers along the side ways. In between the large patches of lawn, there were long trees that were planted randomly, and these provided pleasant shade in summer. The atmosphere around these gardens were very comfortable and relaxing.

There was also ample space for parking our cars, this was a budget well spent.

Towards the end of April the following year, there was much talk going on in the offices of the government of the day, concerning the structuring of the constitution for the newly reborn country which was being chaired by Mr. Khubukonyana a well known politician. There were several topics which were up for discussion and amongst them was the lockout clause which was entrenched in the government's policy, which dealt mainly with striking labourers. I paid special attention to this topic over the radio and television news as this topic was being thoroughly analyzed.

I immediately recognized it as another apartheid instrument which was then used to oppress the country's masses.

A few days later the leaders of the trade unions organized a protest march to that effect. I decided that I would join the masses as I viewed this to be a valuable course. I had always joined these protest marches as I would take leave from work to avoid any disruptions.

The day of the protest march was on a Tuesday, the 30th April and the following day was worker's day, the 1st May. The protest march started promptly with the relevant placards well displayed and by midday the memorandum had been handed over to the official for labour relations. The whole procedure was completed with no disruptions from the police force, who would be shooting at the masses with so-called rubber bullets which pierced the skin and caused severe damage to the tissues. It turned out to be a peaceful march and people dispersed peacefully.

I resumed work on a Thursday which was the 2nd May, I was busy with my work, when my manager called me to his office. In fact he did mention a few words about the day's leave that I had signed. It seemed very awkward, because in his own words on several occasions he did say that, whenever I had private matters to attend, he recommended that I took leave and need not ask for permission. Now in this case why did he question this leave?, as I walked down the stairs to his office, I could feel some perspiration accumulating on my forehead. The reality of this situation was that whenever me and my manager met, it would invariably be a confrontational situation, we rarely met to just share ideas or just enjoy a light conversation, hence my feeling of apprehension.

I walked into his office and was offered a chair opposite him, I said Hi, I should have asked him about his trip overseas, but the situation was not conducive. He started off by telling me that he knew that the day in question had been earmarked for a strike, I said "yes", and he continued to ask me whether I was intimidated to join the strike. This question happened to be amongst some of them that cluttered my mind as I was coming down the stairs earlier on. My immediate reaction I thought to myself, that this kind of mindset had to be calibrated once and for all.

I then proceeded to inform him that I was indeed a member of a trade union and that it was my prerogative to participate in such gatherings. I watched as his face changed from being in control to that of being doubtful, as he finally admitted that he was unsure of company policy in regards labourers going on strike and that he would consult the human resource manage. I have to stress how much I enjoyed this (toyi-toyi) protest march that was without any harassment, intimidation or threats nor disruptions from the powers that be and above all for me, to witness my boss's feeling of insecurity.

Whilst in his office I saw it fit to discuss other matters that concerned my day to day dealings, amongst them was the allocation of my budget which he controlled. What annoyed me was that every time, payments for services rendered to the research division were due, I had to ask for a pay-cheque from him or the marketing director. I interpreted this as saying to me the company does not trust you and yet I handled highly confidential company information. This proved to be a *no go area*, to this day I never enjoyed the privilege to control my own budget, thus no accountability, whether I under or over spent was supposed to be of no concern to me.

Another issue was that I was tired of being humiliated in the presence of other managers, by him uttering words like "Oh! she does not know how to write out sands language (sands language pertains to specific codes used for requesting marketing data from Frankfurt-Germany electronically). I told him that in the past few weeks I had worked hard with the help of the I.S.C. consultants in order for me to be fully conversant with all the requirements, and that he was a bit outdated. Whenever we had these sort of confrontations, my boss would wear this weird kind of smile, and on this particular day he again wore the infamous smile. I left his office feeling very content with myself.

The managers and the executives would go away on business trips without even informing me, neither on their return would they think of giving me a feedback as to our company's performance in relation to our counter parts in the rest of the pharmaceutical world. Whenever the managers were due for these trips, they would leave behind volumes and volumes of work on my e-mail to keep me occupied. This kind of attitude once more raised questions like, "what does a black woman know about market shares?, probably, these meant nothing to her, after all this is a white/male's domain." During these times the temptation to try and escape from this white/male dominated, self-created castle became even more immense, but what kept me going was my desire to see our children through their educational careers.

There seemed to be a high turnover of staff and there were several new people being employed on a regular basis, some were employed as consultants, these positions were accompanied by new cars. One of these consultants, was dealing with wholesalers, and he seemed to be interested in my job and his interest seemed to increase when he heard that I was dealing a lot with price analysis. A few weeks later the company had price increases for all our products. He then came into my office and enquired as to which companies did I notify concerning our price changes. I made it clear that, I notified the relevant software companies, and the wholesalers and they in turn notified the other relevant parties. I least suspected that he had ulterior motives, he complained about how inefficiently this task was done, and if I could do it. I was tempted to refuse out right, but on second thought I decided to try it out. This proved to be a total disaster with bad repercussions. I decided to write him a letter, explaining in details as to why I would no longer pursue this path, and I further cross copied my boss, and the marketing director.

I judged that he saw this black woman and as many a white man, he thought that he had some kind of authority over me.

This letter was further cross copied to all the top managers according to their rank and file, I imagined how embarrassed he must have felt.

This gives me the latitude to reminisce about my schooling days, about matters that happened many, many years gone by, in many high schools. This was when every senior student used to think that they had some authority over the junior students. These seniors would command the juniors to take care of their school books, this meant ensuring that their school books were covered with brown paper and a plastic outer cover and to be ready for class the following day. This was common practice which was done at the beginning of each year. When one refused or when the job was badly done, in turn one would be subjected to very harsh treatment and nobody would intervene, and if one dared to report the matter, this would only aggravate the situation.

A few days later I met him in the foyer, he promptly told me that he had received my e-mail, and he would be replying soon, a few months down the line, I was still waiting.

Amongst the new employees there was a black medical doctor who had qualified at one of the top ranking Universities in the country. I was one of the people who went to her office to welcome her, I was truly excited to have another black woman in our midst. A few months later, I met her in the foyer, I could immediately detect that something was wrong, she had this unhappy looking face. A few months later we then went on a mid-cycle meeting and I was astounded by what I saw, the personal assistant to the medical director treated her with total disdain and displayed very little respect for her.

On our return to work she was then re-allocated to work in the marketing department, this too did not last for long, then she was once more re-allocated to the sales department, where she was expected to carry a briefcase to become a fully fledged sales representative. Hostility towards her from the managers was being clearly reflected as she was trying to knock on every door available, with very little success. What was worse, none of the top executives intervened as I helplessly watched as she was being (shunted) tossed from pillar to post. She had also started to complain bitterly and that the changes that were made affected her salary in a very negative way. I could not be less accurate if I said she hardly stayed with the company for one year, but all what I remember is that her stay was very short.

These were some of the dark days and sad incidences that I witnessed as being some of the changes that were initiated by the c.e.o., but unfortunately it was a total failure.

CHAPTER VIII

Supporting my community

The company was gradually drifting into a phase of work, work, work and becoming less and less people orientated. Members of the management team sat at their computers and laptops until late, some preferred to start work much earlier, the families were forgotten, whilst the race was on. I instantly recognized this scenario, dating back some twenty odd years ago, but in a completely different environment.

There was so much stress expressed on those faces, there seemed to be just too much work for too few a people. However in order for the work to be done such sacrifices were made on a daily basis. Productivity was a word that was thrown around randomly, to me this was a very spiteful word, like "get off your behinds or back sites and start to work more effectively and efficiently". During these hard times the family had taken a back seat, the wife missed her beloved husband, the children had forgotten their father's voice because they seldom heard it of lately.

Staff turn-over was increasing by the numbers, people expressed a lot of dissatisfaction, a lot more baffled faces that were worn by unhappy people, were being seen going about their duties, for them it was business as usual. The path had suddenly become very narrow and the goals less achievable.

Over the years during the struggle against apartheid, 80% of the news reported in the media, were only bad news, (.e.) people being maimed, suicides being committed, the father who murdered his whole family, x-numbers of terrorists being killed in Maputo, Lesotho or Swaziland or in any of the neighbouring African states (e.t.c), this had become a daily phenomenon in the country. The members of the bereaved families mourned and soon they would try to forget as life had to go on and staff members of my company were no exception.

Death struck twice within a short period of two months within the company. The one was a sales team manager and the other was a newly appointed training manager for the company, his responsibility was the training of all the newly employed sales representatives. These deaths shocked the company, and me in particular, because I last witnessed a dying person, taking the last gasp, some twenty-odd years ago, whilst I was a nursing sister. I asked myself several questions, (e.g.) "was there anyone to resuscitate them, did anyone render the final spiritual support, or was there anyone at their side, just to hold their hands and reassuring them, indirectly saying, *you are not alone, we are here for you*, or did they individually just died a lonely death?".

There was lots of talk around the causative factors of death. This was mere speculation, but seemingly stress was ranked as causative factor number one, as these were young men, whose ages ranged between thirty and thirty-four years (30-34) they were at the prime of their lives, at the height of their careers and life had a lot more to offer and yet their lives were cut short so soon. The respective families mourned the loss of their beloved son and brother, sons of the African soil.

A wife mourned the loss of her beloved husband, the children were still too young to understand that they were no longer going to see their beloved daddy, nor hear his voice no more, and the company was saddened by the loss of their employee. Life had taken a turn for the worst for these bereaved families. "May their souls rest in peace".

On the 16th August there were problems in our residential area, barricades were set up at all exits/entrances to our area, everyone was forced to attend a meeting, whereby the erection of squatter camps in our area was to be discussed.

I had read about this issue in the *Sechaba sa Basotho*, a local newspaper that had a high readership amongst the black community. This was a newspaper that was vigilant and had fought the apartheid regime through the might of a pen for many years and only reported the truth to the masses. In short, I trusted this newspaper so much that when I realized that some of the residents had decided to revoke this issue, I immediately volunteered to join forces with them.

Five years into democracy some of the apartheid apparatus were still very much operational, the voiceless masses were still struggling and fighting very hard to have their voices heard.

I notified my boss, that I would be absent from work. Apparently the residents had, had countless meetings with the council officials of the local municipality for the Gauteng region, and all efforts proved futile. On this particular day a mass action campaign was organized by the task force, who consisted of the representatives of our residential area to meet the council officials. The group met down the road which was not far from the area in question and the council officials arrived promptly. Having inspected the area in question, we all then proceeded to a tribunal court which was held at the civic center in Gauteng.

I had never in my lifetime attended anything like this, the council officials sat at the top benches facing us below, the benches were arranged in a circular manner like in a conference room. The chairman addressed us and explained the court proceedings which were to be adhered to throughout. Members of the town planners were also part of the tribunal court, they started off by presenting the infrastructures planned for the area which was soon to be developed as a residential area. This presentation lasted almost the whole morning, conflict arose when the housing department official notified us that they intended relocating people from a nearby squatter camp to our area. The area which was earmarked for relocation of those destitute people, the question was, "Was it suitable for human occupation?", because this area was situated at the bottom end of our area, in a mountainous area.

On rainy days water would slope down to soak this clay-type of soil at the bottom end of this area. The matter was discussed in depth for more than two hours, however the day turned out to be a fruitful one, because the council officials had decided to postpone their plans and promised to review the matter at a later date.

The following day I went back to work, I reported for duty to my manager, who in turn asked me to write a motivational letter and explain in detail, what had transpired on the day in question. I told him that I would prefer signing a leave form, he insisted that I wrote a short motivational letter and suggested it would save me a day.

I had quite a busy day ahead of me, I had to prepare presentations for visitors from our mother body overseas. Visitors from our mother body was a regular scene and this meant that I had to prepare lots of slides for the presentations for my boss, the marketing director, and sometimes the c.e.o. (company executive officer) as well. This was one of those days when we were expecting our v.i.p. (very important people) on whom the continued existence of our company in South Africa depended on. I had been away for one day, just in time to prepare for the presentations, everyone was waiting on me. Having done everybody else's presentations. I then had to focus on my other duty which was by the way another task that I was frequently being reminded, which was that of being a support system to the product managers.

Later on during the afternoon the marketing director, brought the visitors through to our offices to meet us, to my astonishment he passed my office with his back towards my office door, as if trying to block me out of the visitors' sight. Unfortunately or fortunately I looked up simultaneously as the visitors were peeping to try and see their supposed host, but the person who was responsible for introducing them was already ahead and was ready to introduce them to other staff members. This left me flabbergasted, as I least expected this kind of behavior from this man in particular, who once claimed that he fought against the apartheid regime over a number of years. Several questions crossed my mind, were those just words that were being said to try and gain favoritism from people of colour or was there any genuine meaning attached. This question needed further probing, but how do I go about that without ruffling any feathers?, the bare truth was, did the visitors know that 60% of the presentations that were shown to them, less than an hour ago, were prepared by this black woman? On the other hand was the marketing director just being negligent? or was the role that I played within the company insignificant?

Only the following day, did I find some time to re-think about the motivational letter, what came to the fore, was why the interest and the keenness to try and save me a day's leave?. Signing a day's leave was appropriate to me, because what I did during my leave was strictly private. My boss obviously did not embrace this idea.

I had earlier viewed the matter more carefully, the pro's and con's, so I was fully prepared to handle the situation. My response was a simple one. I proceeded to inform him, that to date I had worked for the company for five years, and according to company policy I accumulated one and a two-thirds (1.66) days monthly and to date I had twenty working days due to me per annum and on this note there was absolutely no need for this frugality. I doubt if he expected this poor mathematical calculation, thus topic was closed, thanks to my teacher who tried to teach me a bit of mathematics some thirty-odd years ago.

On this particular day we were attending the usual Monday morning meeting, plans for the forthcoming national sales conference were discussed at random, some reference to the previous sales conferences were made, totally ignoring me. I felt like excusing myself, however I managed to control my emotions. Various emotions swelled up inside of me, the similitude of this situation resembled that of a simmering pot with a tight lid on. The room had suddenly become too small, it felt like the oxygen in the room was just not enough for us all. I thought to myself, I had been shunned from attending the national sales conferences for the past two years, and yet here they were discussing about conferences without any sensitivity.

Towards the end of this meeting my boss, told me that I might be joining the team for the national sales conference and that I would probably be presenting some slides on the new product.

He was saying this with that infamous weird smile which was partially evident on the corner of his lips, accompanied by an anxious look on his face. I could detect that he expected me to glow with excitement, instead I kept my cool and nodded my head as an acknowledgement.

This left him with a question mark, was the acknowledgement for the opportunity granted, or was it directed to the special efforts made on his part, that at last I was eventually allowed to attend overseas conferences once more.

On my very first national sales conference, I had to present some slides on the launch of another new product, remember that I had been debarred from attending conferences for sometime. I had become a bit outdated and out of touch.

Two weeks prior, we had gone on a skills presentation course and a few days later I had to present my slides on the new product to the sales and marketing team. This was like a trial run. Initially making eye contact was a great distraction for me, so I was taught to do this process very selectively, another issue was the use of the electronic pointer and that I should also remember to leave time for questions. All these aspects were sufficiently attended to and this made me feel much more confident and ready to present at the national sales conference.

The second day at the national sales conference I was the second presenter after lunch, these sessions were nicknamed graveyard sessions, because the audience who had just had their lunch, were now feeling drowsy. This meant that my presentation had to be very much stimulating and probably be punctuated by a few jokes, to try and keep them awake.

I started off with a few problems, the microphone was not properly attached to my top (blouse) which meant that I was partially audible, my remote control was a bit slow in bringing up the slide as arranged on my presentation and my hand was shaking so badly that I could not point at the figures on the histograms, adrenalin was pumping through my veins and I was also becoming very anxious.

Never the less following a few seconds I managed to settle down a bit, but I still was not in full control.

I managed gradually to resume charge and proceeded with the presentation and finally I had reached my last slide and it was time for questions. I could feel the sweat running down my spine with my top sticking to my back.

Shortly after my presentation it was tea break, I was actually surprised as some members of the audience congratulated me, some commented on the content of the subject which they said was very informative.

I later thought to myself, that some members of the audience were either scared or felt some empathy for me, hence some members preferred to ask me questions during the tea break.

The company had appointed a new training manager, I was excited with this appointment, because I knew him very well. Our relationship dated back to when I was first employed by the company. We (the training manager and myself) belonged to the same team and we worked mainly in the government hospitals. We only met during PCM, MCM and during national sales conferences (pre and mid-cycle meetings) as mentioned that during these meetings, we would team up in groups to discuss our products and marketing strategies.

The training manager and myself shared lots of ideas, we had a lot in common, he was smart, he was hard working and he did not hesitate to pinpoint the pitfalls that he encountered as a hospital sales representative. He lived and worked in Cape Town and his country trip was in Transkei, of which he felt was a waste of fuel, time and resources. He thought that his colleague who lived and worked in Durban could work in the area as it was much nearer. These were some of the issues that we encountered that contributed to the company's inadequate management style.

On his appointment as the new training manager, he identified several areas that needed innovation and implementation. He created a new format for the training of newly employed sales representatives, he reorganized the set-up for hosting the PCM and MCM meetings. Amongst other issues which were of concern to him was my position of the market research officer. He said that the average sales representative was unsure of my role within the marketing department. They probably thought that I was an assistant to my boss and sometimes served him with tea. He highlighted matters that were obscure to me at the time, but pertinent to my development as a market research officer. In order for the sales representatives to know my role I needed to feature somewhere during the course of their training. On his next program he would include me as one of the presenters and be part of the managers responsible for the training of the newly employed representatives. I appreciated this notion, the sales representatives would be able to identify with me, they would be able to consult me in regards issues that concerned their areas. My task during this training session, would be to educate them on my role within the company. This was my opportunity to teach them on how the market shares were done, how the prescription information was collected, how the call rates were compiled and finally how all the above affected their performance.

A brief explanation on the market shares;

(A) The market shares by company, meant that, the total value of all the pharmaceutical companies in South Africa were added together to make a total sum of money in rands and dollars. Then each company's value would be divided into the total sum obtained for the total pharmaceutical companies/market, this would then be converted to a percentage, and this would then be the market share for the individual company.

The market shares were further broken down by product, and also by the newly introduced products to the market, which were considered as being new only for the first twenty four (24) months. Market shares are valuable tools for the company, but as one marketer once remarked, "market shares are there to boost one's ego, but unfortunately they cannot be saved/stored with the financial institutions".

(B) The prescriptions market; the data collecting company (I.S.C.) kept records of the medical practitioner's written prescriptions by area and by product, this data is collected from four hundred (400) medical practitioners per quarter and this data would then be multiplied by two (2), thus formulating a six (6) monthly data on prescriptions. The group of four hundred (400) medical practitioners were being rotated quarterly to ensure an even distribution of prescription data. The relevance of this data for the sales representative, was to detect which areas were weak or strong in terms of generating prescriptions for the company's products.

(C) The call rate market; The data collecting company analyzed the calls, by the number of calls, by the duration of the call and the quality of the call, they also kept records of the medical practitioner whereby information was gathered quarterly pertaining to the analysis as stated above. The use of this information for the sales representative would be to evaluate her/his performance in the area, (e.g.) if the quality of the call was rated three (3), this would then mean a poor detail of the product to the medical practitioner, and a poor detail did not generate prescriptions.

My presentation would then last for forty to fifty (40-50) minutes, which included a detailed explanation on the use of the price analysis list, which required regular updates due to the dynamics of the pharmaceutical market.

I really appreciated this innovation from him, it helped me to improve on my presentation skills, especially the aspect of eye contact and this also taught me to anticipate for probable questions and to have answers readily available. This exercise proved to be beneficial to both parties (the audience and myself) as it alleviated the tension.

My relationship with the training manager was now re-established, since we both were residing in Johannesburg/Gauteng and he was readily available to listen to my complaints. I now had a big brother within the company, whenever I encountered problems with my boss or the human resource manager, he would be the first one to know and he would always encourage me to stay positive and not allow them to break me.

It was not only always gloomy, but there were certain days that brought about lots of laughter and joy amongst the company employees.

The company had an events coordinator, whose main task was to ensure that all employees of the company would meet on a social level. These consisted of beer-festivals which were organized on Saturdays, whereby we would all sit on the beautiful lawn, with some music in the background, enjoying some snacks and some drinks.

During major soccer events, the c.e.o. would invite us all to assemble in the canteen to watch international soccer games on a large television screen. Snacks and drinks would be served all on company costs.

The events coordinator would also organize a golf-day for our clients (medical doctors) to play against the company managers. In preparation for this sporting event, T-shirts, caps and golf-balls with the company logo displayed on them, these would be given to each and every participant on that day. The company would invite my husband to join them as part of the management team. My husband really appreciated this gesture and always looked forward to sharing the day with the management team.

These events had a special impact on me, I often wondered to myself as to why could this pleasant atmosphere not have a spin-off on to our working relationship.

On other days there would be certain events that were organized by the media, for every citizen to participate. These events were commonly known as *walk the talk*. The company's events coordinator would once more make sure that T-shirts and caps with the company logo displayed, were issued to each and every participant. The media organizers would then offer prizes to the various winners, and our company would also offer snacks and drinks to all the participants. These were real fun days for those who enjoyed the race.

Having been in this job for several years, I had perfected my skills, my monthly reports were written in such an expressive and elaborate manner that the marketing director, was impressed and decided to forward his copy to the c.e.o.

He too was impressed and requested that he be included in the following month's mailing list. My boss, apparently was not particularly pleased with this, so he suggested that before dispatching the reports, they should be assessed by him for approval. Unfortunately the very, very first time, when the reports were ready and due to be dispatched, my boss was away on business and the reports had to be dispatched as usual, omitting the c.e.o., pending my boss's approval. Again the marketing director did forward his copy to the c.e.o. In response to this, the c.e.o. released a strong worded letter directed at me and my boss stating the importance for him in receiving his own copy. Once more my boss was not very pleased with this, as this reflected his autocratic style of management.

A newly appointed junior product manager joined the marketing team early during the year. I knew him as a sales representative, we got along very well, we had a few things in common and we often shared similar positive views. I was one of those who extended a warm welcome to him. I also orientated him and reassured him about my availability to assist. It did not take him long to settle in with the rest of the members of the marketing team.

I was astonished to receive an e-mail from him, in my view the contents of the e-mail were derogative. This e-mail was in circulation, every employee of the company had received it with an exception of the company executives. Having read the e-mail, I expected someone from the ranks of the managers to act promptly, but days passed, without any remedial action. As the days passed by, I could no longer contain my anguish, I decided to send an e-mail to my boss, and again the days continued to pass by, without any response. This issue was now causing me sleepless nights, each time I was faced with him I would think to myself, "what was going on in this young man's mind?", I felt compelled to do something, to prevent issues of a similar nature from reoccurring. I then decided to consult the training manager, as mentioned, he had become my big brother within the company, I asked for his opinion on the contents of the e-mail, he too found the e-mail to be very offensive. The contents of the e-mail consisted of portraits of several men, who were working on their computers, but they wore masks of baboons. The training manager, remarked that a similar e-mail with the same contents had been in circulation a few months after our democracy, it had caused an uproar in the offices of ruling political party.

The question was, "What was this youngman trying to do?"

Several days later I decided to report the matter to the human rights commissioner, who was equally astonished and flabbergasted that such e-mails were still in circulation at this century. He then set up a meeting with my boss, the contents of the meeting were kept confidential, but what I appreciated, was the apology extended directly to me by my boss and another apology which was sent to all employees of the company via e-mail.

On the day of the apology, 1 could recall my boss walking into my office, with a very serious, unhappy look on his face, which I later interpreted as a gesture of disappointment and embarrassment.

Relations between me and my boss, seemed strained. The week prior his departure, he was going on a business trip overseas.

I managed to send him a farewell note via e-mail, to which he responded positively, however on his return he was too occupied, he could not even just say Hi! to me, he seemed to be on cloud nine. I presumed that he probably had to give a detailed feedback to the company executives, hence his state of being pre-occupied. This type of reaction was not unfamiliar, invariably I would choose to ignore and continue with my work as usual.

CHAPTER IX

Conflict of interest

My workload was steadily increasing, I had to do sands-run (electronic request for data from the surveillance company) to Frankfort in Germany. This consisted of sands language which mostly comprised of special codes, and due to the time difference between the two countries, I could only send e-mails late in the afternoon. In short I would write out the request and store it in a special folder, ready for dispatch. My computer was also gradually giving me problems, the memory was also running out, this resulted in frequent shutdowns, sometimes my computer would shutdown (crush) whilst I was in the process of downloading data from Frankfort. I would report this to my boss as the i.t. (information technology) support team were getting tired of re-booting my computer almost every second day. The memory was upgraded a few times, but due to the extensive amount of data and other data from various software companies, I still experienced the same problem. The situation was becoming unbearable, as I watched newly appointed managers being issued with new computers, the question arose, "was this discrimination?, was the job that I do, not important?, or bears no value to the company, so why keep me?"

One morning I had data sent to me from one of the software companies, as I was busy downloading the material onto my hard drive, my computer decided to shutdown, this infuriated me.

I immediately reported this to my boss. I waited in anticipation for his prompt response, instead he completely forgot about me.

I then decided to report this to the marketing director, who was equally occupied, I then decided to send him an e-mail. I felt helpless, adrenalin combined with anger was surging through my veins, the albatross of oppression around my neck, had become too heavy for me to carry.

There was only one option available at my disposal at the time, and that was to leave my desk and to find solace somewhere and that was, the place I called my home, and risk being dismissed in absentia.

Somehow I had to draw someone's attention to my plight, I also needed space to clear my mind. Driving home at that time of the day, the road seemed very long and lonely, it was as if I was the only motorist on the road, unlike in the mornings, whereby the traffic would be very busy. This allowed my mind to really go wild, as several questions crowded my mind, I thought to myself, "was this how my career was to end?" Tears were rolling down my cheeks, I had to wipe them with the back of my hand as they were obscuring my vision. I got home, found our eldest son, he could detect that something was wrong. I had parked my car in the driveway, instead of parking it inside the garage. He came up to me and told me that someone from my workplace had phoned and left a message that I should phone him immediately on my arrival. I was still pondering over this message, when the phone rang, our son looked at me as if saying "go ahead and answer, it must be from the same person who has been looking for you from your work place." Instead of answering the phone, anger and rage instantly took control, I disconnected the phone, I desperately needed to be alone. I needed time to think things over, "was I going to give them the upper hand? and what would be the best thing to do under these circumstances?" I sat alone in our bedroom, I wondered as to what my father's reaction would have been to this debacle. Well I had a pretty fair idea; "Matema pitja e, ke kgale o i loyisha, byale go shetje gore o sole gore o je" "Matema you have been stirring this pot for a very long time, it is finally ready, waiting for you to dish-up and eat" It suddenly dawned on me that I had behaved in the most cowardly manner by me running away.

I thought to myself that I had been an old member of the trade union and I had never utilized their services before and this would be an appropriate time, my job was in jeopardy.

I stayed home for two days, on the third day I made arrangements to return to work with a representative from the Trade Unions organization, who was to assist me in handling the matter. During my brief to the Trade Union representative, he was actually surprised that it took me such a long time before I realized that I needed some intervention.

On my return to work, I was given an official letter addressed to me, notifying me to attend a disciplinary enquiry. The date, time and venue were clearly stipulated. I was also informed that, should I fail to attend the disciplinary enquiry for whichever reason, the enquiry would proceed without me. This sounded very threatening, though I had already told myself that I had to be present, with or without a representative, I needed this opportunity whereby I would be able to state my case.

A disciplinary hearing was arranged that excluded my representative from the trade unions, this upset me very much.

The trade unionist on the other hand wanted to force issues by obtaining a special permission from the authorities to represent me. This I did not approve of, I did not want a showdown or a display of who was wielding the greatest power, because in my view, the fact of the matter was that I was still an employee of the company, which meant that I had to respect their decisions.

I then proceeded to ask my colleague who was the manager of two (2) black representatives, he declined in a tactful manner, I knew that he feared the repercussions and victimization that would follow. I was now on my own, I thought to myself, I need to fight this fight to the bitter end.

The meeting started promptly, chaired by the human resource manager, present was my boss, myself and the human resource manager's personal assistant. I was given the opportunity to start off the proceedings, and then followed by my boss. We were both (i.e.) my boss and myself given a chance to state our cases and there was sufficient time for questioning by the company representative. My boss and I sat on opposite sides of the table, facing each other, what amazed me, was that during this whole process we did not make any eye contact. The question was "did he know the outcome/verdict before hand?"

The outcome turned out not to be in my favour, to me the entire saga was biased as the core of the problem, (ie) my computer was left un-tackled, instead company policy was being reiterated.

This saga had turned out to be the talk of the town, almost everybody was following the case closely. My colleagues who were also closely watching the situation, were probably wondering to themselves, "why was I tolerating this abuse?" The similarity of this situation was that of an abused spouse, quote "The abused spouse who keeps on returning to the arms that were once warm and loving, but had since gone cold and distant".

Allow me to share my sentiments from a speech by a politician, "the oppressor and exploiter would strive to be on top for all times, while the down-trodden would struggle to stand on their feet".

Two weeks later, It was month-end, and I had not been paid my monthly salary, when I enquired I was referred to the human resource manager, remember, our relationship was nothing worth mentioning and I always wished for minimal crossing of our paths. I dreaded this encounter, however circumstances forced me to confront him, with very little success.

Following repeated attempts, my salary was eventually released via my boss, this too was not a pleasant encounter.

A few days later the whole saga was reported to the marketing director, in writing. I preferred relating my story on paper, the reason being that I did not want to omit anything important.

Six months down the line, I had had no response from the marketing director, in the mean time my boss's attitude towards me was appalling. I was then left with one more option, (i.e.) to take one more risk and report the matter to the c.e.o.

This too was done after a prolonged deliberation with myself.

I then wrote a letter to the c.e.o. with all the details of the enquiry, how I judged the outcome to have been biased. It was a very comprehensive letter, and I made sure that nothing was mistakenly omitted. The highlights were the manner in which the disciplinary enquiry was conducted, the outcome and finally the repercussions, which were very negative.

Following several attempts to secure an appointment with the c.e.o., I was finally granted the opportunity, of which I was very grateful.

On the day of the appointment, I had prepared my case as best as I could, especially the issue of the with-holding of my salary, as to me this was a most despicable act, it infringed on my rights as an employee of the company and which would bear negative consequences for the company if exposed.

On my arrival at the c.e.o's office, I found him busy with his work and a few minutes later he was available, the human resource manager was called in to be part on the meeting.

The greeting was abrupt and he looked tense, the next statement was negative, as his approach was, quote "what's your problem?" I thought to myself, what a manner to address a sensitive issue of this nature. He offered me a seat, I had just started to relate my story and he immediately took charge. He went on a tangent for almost two minutes, telling me that he had no regard for trade unions, and that he could pay me a six month's salary without any hassles. He continued with the verbal abuse, and he asked me, what was so special about me, that makes me think that I could just write him a letter and challenge him. He also told me in no uncertain terms that should my act be repeated, I would be dismissed instantly and that he would make sure that I leave the company in such a manner that my feet would not be able to touch the ground, and when he was done with me, I would not know what hit me.

This kind of utterances, I interpreted, as a demonstration of how much power he wielded (i.e.) hiring and firing as he pleased, to me this was no reflection of a multinational company.

I had to intervene because, in my opinion the main objective of the meeting was being overlooked, inwardly I told myself that I was not leaving his office without telling him my side of the story.

I sighed with relief, when I was finally granted the opportunity to state my case. The human resource manager sat next to me and was as quiet as a church mouse. During the argument I kept a close watch on his reactions, I could see his facial expression gradually becoming lighter, his facial brow also began to relax and the tone of his voice was calming down, the rest I could not detect, maybe he managed to hide them from me successfully. Otherwise the human resource manager only answered questions that were directed at him, whilst we (i.e.) the c.e.o. and myself dominated the meeting, and at the end I was able to tell him how much I appreciated the positive changes that came about within the company during his reign. I saw it fit to inform him that, even my promotion to the current position, I knew for a fact that his influence was a contributing factor. I also told him that he had great visions for the future of the company, however the question was, "did his managers share this vision with him?", this comment did not go down so well with him. I also took this opportunity to inform him of all my grievances, because my sixth sense kept on telling me, that this opportunity might never come my way ever again, hence the need for full exploitation.

As the dialogue continued, the tension was gradually evaporating, and was being gently replaced by an amount of calamity. We started chatting like old friends who were kept apart for a long time. He also said that he was glad that someone within the company was able to see him as a friend and could come to him when in need. This statement was very reassuring. After a prolonged dialogue, the meeting ended on a more positive note, whereby he asked me that in future I should direct my complaints to the marketing director, whom he felt that I should have consulted in the first place.

As mentioned I seldom spoke to this English man, hence the reluctance. Once more, the core of the matter (problematic computer) was left unaddressed, I was now doubtful as to whether this matter would ever be resolved.

My mind was very pre-occupied, as whether to resign or not, when I received a telephone call from the c.e.o, the tone of his voice was very gentle, though firm, he insisted that I spoke to the marketing director, the background noise were denotative of aircrafts, which told me that he was at the airport ready to embark on one of his business trips overseas, and yet there he was concerned about my situation, this humbled me.

When I finally got to the marketing director's office, I could clearly depict that he had been expecting me. He had a subtle way of saying "I am listening", by him taking a writing pad and making notes of the conversation, I admired this gesture. I then proceeded to relate my story once more and all my grievances, he then promised to view the whole situation and promised to give me feedback in due course.

A few days later by boss was trying to scold me for the action that I had taken, I told him that I was made to believe that the c.e.o. had an open-door policy and that I thought of utilizing it.

Six months later as I anticipated for a feedback from the c.e.o. or the marketing director or even my boss, I could witness a few positive changes. I was included in most meetings which were pertinent to my job, being excluded from attending the national sales conference was something of the past, even my boss's attitude towards me changed for the better.

My life was gradually beginning to stabilize and I thought that I needed a holiday. I decided to visit the U.S.A. I was accompanied by my daughter and my grand-daughter. We spent one week in New York in the big city, we visited most of the historic places and another few days were spent by the countryside (Great Barrington) and the last few days in Boston.

I recalled that with my previous company, we would spend sometime at the J.F.K. airport waiting for a connecting flight to Philadelphia where the headquarters were situated and I often yearned to just get onto the streets of New York and do some shopping. This time it was a pleasure to alight from the plane and get on to the streets of New York, to catch a cab. This city was a gigantic version of Johannesburg, in terms of the geographical size and the population density. At a mere glance one could see the enormity of the city, it is an ideal tourist destination. We stood for a few minutes just to watch the hustle and bustle, people just going about their daily lives as if there was no tomorrow.

One of the evenings we went to watch the Boston symphony orchestra in action, this was a dream come true for me. Shopping was irresistible, remember these were women and shopping is almost every woman's best friend.

One of the days we took a cab to the border of Canada and the U.S.A. to witness the Niagara falls. I had only seen this on a postcard that was sent to me by a friend, who then lived in Toronto, Canada. On our arrival, we were amazed by the beauty of this scenery, water flowing, endlessly down a very large sized river, simultaneously reflecting rainbow colours. We just stood there in awe from the afternoon till the early hours of the morning, we could not just see enough of this creation by God.

We took pictures from every angle of the Niagara Falls, the view at night was even more spectacular.

A quote from card # 1'travel & sightseeing' series.

Niagara Falls at Night: "The Niagara River", which forms a natural border between the U.S. and Canada, delivers water from Lake Erie at 570 feet above sea level to lake Ontario at 243 feet. Niagara Falls is a spectacular "Lee Age" geological creation formed around 10,000B.C.

It is considered to be one of the "seven Natural Wonders of the world". "Millions of visitors each year stand in awe when they see this masterpiece".

This was another memorable scenery for me as I just stood there watching the waters rushing down the various layers of mountains down to the Niagara river and that in September, 1998 we were actually part of the millions who witnessed one of the natural wonders of the world.

Once more I could not resist comparing what we saw some six thousand miles away, with what we had back home in Africa. The Victoria falls in Zimbabwe was a miniature version of the Niagara falls.

We slept over as we retired late and we also wished to visit the museum and to see some of the indigenous people of the land (the red Indians).

We really enjoyed every moment, thus the holiday was well spent as a result I was mentally and physically ready to resume work.

CHAPTER X

Reaping the fruits

Things were happening so swiftly that I began to wonder, whether this was still the same company? Oh yes, it was, except that the company was being managed in style "Bathopele" "*people first*". We once more had black receptionists in the front desk, one was disabled, but the company had granted her an equal opportunity for employment. A black product manager was appointed, this type of position was only reserved for whites, sadly the job reservation act had fallen away in the new dispensation. The atmosphere had changed, it was like viewing the flip side of the same coin, the young group of aspiring university graduates, that were mentioned earlier on, were now fully fledged managers, who were prepared to take the company forward. These were hard working, determined young men who had foresight into the future.

Within a time span of two to three years, there were many changes, some top managers were being transferred to head office, junior managers were being promoted to the top positions, my boss happened to be amongst them.

I subsequently moved to another office and a bit far away from the hustle and bustle of the marketing team.

Once more I was reporting to the marketing director, as mentioned he was a cool guy, who was in control in his own way. I was allowed to conduct my part of work as usual with minimal disruptions, which I enjoyed. I had just began to fully appreciate my work, the environment had become more pleasant and friendly. I had also recently received a ten year service award from the company and according to company policy, I was due for a new car. My husband and I thought it wise for me not to opt for a company car, but for me to use our family car. The reason being that he had gone into business and only used the car on weekends. This resulted in huge savings for us, because we only paid for maintenance and major services, the rest was provided by the company.

I fully enjoyed the use of our family car, the downside to this, was that the taxman did not spare us, the money that we thought we were saving was indirectly being paid back to the taxman in various forms.

Three years later, two years before I was due for my fifteenth year's service award, I was being retrenched. I had just turned sixty two years and was anticipating for my retirement in the next few years. I was shocked that this had come much earlier than I had anticipated. It was almost three weeks back following our return from the national sales conference, which meant that we were still partially on cloud nine. This phase was similar to a honeymoon for the marketing team, because marketing strategies were laid out during the national sales conference and the sales representatives were out in the field to try and implement them. Invariably these strategies were for newly launched products, as mentioned that the c.e.o. was very proactive and was forever envisaging for the company to launch new products. My task in this regard was to ensure that the sales representatives had price analysis lists that were up to date.

Now here were these two men in this office that I was called to, I did not know what to expect.

I was at the canteen enjoying breakfast with my colleague, when I was called to the marketing director's office and found the human resource manager. On my arrival I could depict a subtle sense of uneasiness, this kept me guessing.

The human resource manager made the first move, he got up and immediately handed me a letter and also informed me that due to the introduction of the latest technology my services had become redundant.

"WOW, what a blow!", I tried hard to recall the events of that fateful morning as they unfolded. I vaguely remember standing there motionless, not knowing what to say. Inwardly, I had the desire to accept the letter from the human resource manager, but my impulses were delayed for some reasons unknown to me. I could not extend my hand as quickly as I would had desired to.

Due to this unexplainable incident, there was a moment of absolute silence, the three of us were exchanging a strange gaze from one to the other in amazement.

When I eventually managed to reach out to accept the letter from the human resource manager, within a split of a second I managed to detect the sigh of relief from the marketing director. My hand was still trembling from shock, I tried to read the letter, but none made sense to me at the time. My response was that of utter shock. I do not remember, me actually reading the contents of the letter to the very end, my brain cells were suddenly over-loaded with various messages, my head was spinning, I was drowning in my own thoughts. Some were negative and some were positive but the fact of the matter was that this decision by the company had been deliberated for some time, maybe even before we went on the national sales conference, and all I had to do, was to accept it and move on with my life.

I briefly looked at the marketing director once more and I thought to myself, that our ages did not differ much and yet he was allowed to stay on, how unfair.

Following this meeting I had to return to my office, which was down the stairs, only a few minutes walk away, but on this particular day, the trip was endless. I just did not seem to reach my office. My legs seemed too weak to carry me, my knees were no longer all that flexible anymore, age had suddenly caught up with me. When I finally reached my office, I was drenched in my own perspiration, my knees were still shaking. I had to close my office door, so that I could find some time to recover and to delve into my own thoughts.

As I was dwelling in my thoughts, tears were filling my eyes, I had a heavy lump in my throat, I felt like screaming, but would that help? maybe it would, by taking away some of the tension, but I had to control myself. Remember that other part of me, was to be in control, no matter what the circumstances were.

I had never before been exposed to such, remember from my previous employments, I was always the one who decided that I needed to leave for another job, hence this kind of reaction "utter shock".

The letter had covered most of the aspects regarding retrenchment, (e.g.) being told that, should a suitable position arise I would be considered.

Our paths crossed once more again, me and the human resource manager and he seemed to be on the upper hand as I could detect a subtle smile at the corner of his lips, except that he would have been happier if I left the company, much earlier and probably empty handed.

After all these years, it felt like home, my colleagues were like close friends, the black staff in the warehouse were like my own relatives, in short the bond which had been developed over the years with my fellow employees could not be easily broken.

When thinking back to that fateful day, I still could not account for the events that followed thereafter, all I remember, was that time moved too fast and suddenly it was time to knock-off.

When I informed my husband in the evening, I did not know what to expect, but to my surprise, he comforted and supported me. He was much stronger, because he had been through a similar process a few years earlier and that was when he decided to start his own business.

The package was a fairly reasonable one in my opinion, at least we could start by paying off our debts and we were only left with our youngest son, who was still battling with his matriculation.

The rest of the month went by very fast, some of my colleagues responded pleasantly to the news and came to my office to wish me well. I really appreciated the emotional support, and some advices for my retirement.

Having worked for a company for so long, the company was like my second home, except that members of this family were much more extensive.

My very last day was one of the saddest moments that I experienced in a very long time, just to say good-bye, set off more emotional feelings, this was painful, so I decided to send an e-mail, bidding each and everyone farewell, I knew that it would be read by everyone in the company.

Allow me to express my gratitude, that someone did come to my rescue, and to my surprise it was the c.e.o. himself, to this day I applaud the bold decision he took against all odds. Many a manager was granted the opportunity to climb up the ladder within the pharmaceutical industry.

Some went as far as having their careers developed internationally, at no cost of their own. Taking into account that most of these managers were South African males, who were raised under the apartheid regime (i.e.) enhancing white supremacy at all cost, even when we were already living in a democratic society, with a black government in place. However, the c.e.o still continued to pursue his vision for the company, that was to give everyone an equal opportunity.

At the end of the day I was glad that I made a positive decision to stay on and continue with the struggle.

Thirty years down the line, I could still recall how hard, and how often I fell and how quickly I got up, pulled myself together, shook-off the dust and continued on the path that I now call "the struggle of a black woman in a capitalist society".

Any lesson learnt from this? Oh Yes!

That the chances of women in a male dominated world is an ongoing struggle, let alone a black woman.

Remember that one cannot do it alone and the same applies to the other party, who should have the obligation to allow each other to explore their capabilities to achieve their goals.

WOMEN

As women we cry when we are happy
And laugh when we are nervous
We fight for what we believe
And stand up for injustice
We don't take no for an answer,
When we believe there is a better solution.

We go without new shoes so our children can
We go to the doctor with a frightened friend
We love unconditionally
We cry when our children excel
And cheer when a friend gets an award.

We are overjoyed when we hear about a birth
Or new marriage
Our hearts break when a friend dies
We can show our sorrow when we loose a family member
But we are the strongest
When there seems to be no strength left
And we certainly know that a kiss can
Heal any broken wounds.

We come in all colours shapes and sizes
We'll drive, fly, walk or run
Just to show how much we care
The hear of a woman is what makes the world spin
We do more than give birth
We bring love, joy, hope and compassion to
Almost every one
We give moral support to our family and friends
But always remember we do have a lot to say
And a lot to give.

I thought of sharing this message which was in circulation on e-mal

These are synopsis of the letters that I wrote regularly to management.

I had written a letter to my boss complaining about my computer that was not performing and I sent another copy to the it manager and the helpdesk.

I informed management about my frustrations and how pressurized I felt especially during peak times, when I had to meet deadlines and time had to be wasted by having to reboot because of memory errors.

I had become desperate for help and unfortunately there was no one. I once more explained the situation of my computer.

My pc does not meet my needs, 90% of the time it failed me, booting and re-booting is the order of the day, boss, and IT manager, knew about this problem.

The situation had become most unbearable.

The last straw was the morning, when I wanted to print sands runs that I had downloaded from Europe, and my pc failed to operate. The it manager was informed immediately, and I was told to take the negative option, which was to abort the data, and in my view this was not an option.

I had absconded from work, and stayed home for three days.

On my return to work I was summoned to a disciplinary enquiry.

Subsequent to this there was a barrage of correspondence from me to my bosses and including the c.e.o. of the company, it was with intense desperation that I needed for the matter to be resolved.

A brief letter that I wrote to address the disciplinary enquiry.

I like my job and I do enjoy it, except when I experience problems with my computer, which seem endless.

Since then I have been complaining to my manager about the non-performance of my computer.

My computer does not cope with the demands of my work on a daily basis, my manager asked me the previous year to cross copy him whenever I requested help from our helpdesk line to assist me with the problems I encountered with my pc, I believed this was to try and ascertain the extent of the problem.

This was done every time I encountered a problem, my requests were +/-5 a day, now this involved booting and re-booting, which is done on a problematic pc. (a time consuming exercise)

Following this my memory was upgraded, but due to the extent of my work the memory was used up very quickly.

I once more returned to the same problem, I started again to ask for help, either through the help desk line or sometimes I telephoned, depending on the urgency of the work at hand.

Once more nothing was done, I have often watched my fellow employees being promoted into the marketing department and new/competent computers were organized for them.

A fellow colleague once remarked and said that he had lost count as to the number of times he had seen Anne (a member of the help-desk line) frequenting my office, now this is from someone who has occupied the office opposite me for less than three months.

The question at hand is "Do I not deserve a new/competent pc or can my company not afford R5,000 to invest in an employee, or is the work that I do not of any significance?"

To me going through all this was very much unnecessary in the first place, if things were objectively judged/done and appropriate measures taken.

The outcome of the disciplinary enquiry was, that I was given a written warning, I was given no clear explanation for the act of with-holding my salary. I kept on asking myself, "What is the main objective of disciplinary action?"

A synopsis of the letter written addressing the outcome of the disciplinary enquiry.

I would like to refer you to the disciplinary policy as extracted from the labour law relations act (Act 1995) which clearly states that the objective of the whole exercise is to correct the misconduct or to improve work performance, if at all possible, in order that the individual concerned may continue to make an effective contribution to the company.

Discipline should by its very nature be corrective and not punitive; that all employees are treated in a fair and consistent manner. It is essential that disciplinary action must in all cases be consistent, prompt, firm and fair. Another purpose of taking corrective action is not to punish an employee, but to help him/her to get back on track.

After the disciplinary enquiry I expected the human resource manager to set a reasonable date to review the progress.

A referral to my contract with the company, No where does it state that, should there be any misconduct by an employee, that the company will have the right to with-hold an employee's salary.

In view of the above mentioned facts, this is a serious violation of my right as an employee of the company.

The issue at hand was totally disregarded (defective computer)

I would like to put a few things into perspective; I am not fighting, by no means should this be regarded as Matema being up in arms against the company, but I feel that there is a deep need to address the inequalities that are being inflicted upon some of the employees of the company. For example the main cause of the issue at hand, was the inability of my pc, which I felt was not coping with the demands of my job, as explained in my previous letters. I had lodged several complains about my computer, but nothing really of significance was done to sort out the problem. Three years down the line I've been bottling up my feelings of frustration, and on the day in question, I found the situation to be most unbearable, and when I tried to raise my voice, it was like

I'm being told to shut-up and to go and do my job that I'm being paid for.

To me it seemed that I'm being discriminated against, apartheid is supposed to be dead, as you once told us during one of your presentation, but unfortunately at our company it is still very much alive, I'm afraid to say that this element (apartheid) hampers the productivity level of the employees.

There is an urgent need for this situation to be addressed, something has to be done, the executives who are in the upper echelons of the company, need to be aware that we need each other in order to bring about change, and that we have been in the new South Africa some five years ago, and that it is vital that we all play a pivotal role in the democratization of our country.

A letter written to the c.e.o. regarding the outcome of the disciplinary enquiry.

On the day in question, I wished to report this matter to you the c.e.o, unfortunately I was told that you were unavailable.

This is the day I learnt that my salary was being with-held, pending the outcome of the disciplinary enquiry.

I've had a computer problem since my appointment to this position, I've written several letters similar to this one.

A copy was sent to the marketing director, as I felt that I had to report to someone, who might consider my plight on a more serious note, unfortunately the tension was so high that I found myself going home, of which I deeply regret.

Having left my office, I phoned two days later to make an appointment to speak to my boss once more.

I returned to work, with the aim of discussing the issue, I had also organized a representative from the trade union, of which I was denied.

I was then issued with an invitation to attend the disciplinary enquiry to be held in two days-time, the letter was written and the conditions there-of, these were addressed to me.

I was totally dissatisfied with the outcome, in my view the real issue was left un attended and the problem is still unsolved.

On the day in question when I was told that my salary was being with-held pending the outcome of the enquiry, which was held the previous day, I got very upset. I then enquired from the human resource manager, the scene was an unpleasant one, and none of the responses were convincing.

However a pay-cheque with a clearance note were delivered to me late that afternoon, which I deposited through the ATM, as the following day was a public holiday.

Summary, Instead of handling the real problem at hand, rather I am being seen as being the problem.

A summary of the disciplinary policy.
(a version based on the labour law relations—Act 1995)

1. The intent of disciplinary action is to correct misconduct or to improve work performance, if at all possible, in order that the individual concerned may continue to make an effective contribution to the company.

2. Discipline should therefore by its very nature be corrective and not punitive.

3. It is essential that disciplinary action must in all cases be consistent, prompt, fair and firm.

4. Resolutions of any conflict should be settled, where possible, at the lowest possible level, without third party involvement.

5. Parties involved should agree on specific action and follow-up dates

6. If it is decided to take corrective action, the steps as laid out on the disciplinary procedure, should be followed.

GLOSSARY

Apartheid—racial segregation in South Africa .

Aisi—elder sister

Bantu—black people of South Africa

Bantu-stands—designated areas for the black people of South Africa

Bek—mouth of an animal

Bronchodilators—medication that relaxes the smooth muscles of the Airway to facilitate breathing

Deposit—money paid as security .

Dispensing doctor—dual role , that of medical practitioner and a pharmacist.

Dompas—identity document

Gravel road—small stoned path

Home boy—people from the same village

Movie—watched in bioscope/cinema

Pikinini—derogative name for a black child

Prognosis—outcome of an illness/disease

White supremacy—white people having the highest authority

Terrorist—formidable people seen as trouble makers

Toyi-toyi—dance performed during protest march

Vernacular—language of the country .

The constitution of the Republic of South Africa, 1996 (Act 108 of 1996.)

NB. The use of fictitious names to protect the identities of the characters and the real venues, that are quoted in this book.